SEW IT YOURSELF

The author's daughter Lisi poses in
a mini-dress made of an African border
print. The dress is red, purple, and black.

SEW IT YOURSELF

Marylis Muhlhauser

GALAHAD BOOKS · NEW YORK CITY

To my daughters Lisi and Susan
and to Karol Williams

Published by Galahad Books, a division of A & W
Promotional Book Corporation, 95 Madison Ave-
nue, New York, N.Y. 10016, by arrangement with
Henry Regnery Company, 114 West Illinois
Street, Chicago, Ill. 60610

Library of Congress Catalog Card No.: 73-79816
ISBN: 0-88365-035-5

Manufactured in the United States of America.

Contents

Introduction

Clothes designs have never been simpler, but clothes prices are as high as they ever were. Perhaps higher. A ready-made dress, consisting of only a few yards of fabric, may be priced at fifty times its weight in gold. Design, fabric, labor, marketing, and business expenses in general increase the cost of such a dress. In fact, the fabric may be the least expensive item of the garment.

So why not make your own dresses? Why not save the cost of labor and marketing, and most of the cost of the designing? Fabrics can be bought at your favorite store. Fabulous fabrics. A crisp, no-iron summer dress can be made from material costing only three dollars; a pair of slacks, from double-knit wool, for six; a maxi-length slinky jersey jungle print, for ten. Design? Some of the most famous designer names—Yves St. Laurent, Bill Blass, Rudi Gernreich, Hubert de Givenchy—commercialize their patterns. And all pattern costs are minimal.

You can't sew? Now, really. Sewing is not all *that* difficult. If you have average intelligence, if you can make a cake from a recipe in a cookbook, if you can follow instructions, you can sew.

There are one or two skills that must be learned. The rest is a step-by-step process. And practice. Note that there are even instructions on the package of a premix cake. Step-by-step instructions. That is what this book is all about—step-by-step sewing.

M.M.

1

The Preliminaries

Susan models a halter dress in black and white silk. A simple pattern such as this one is a good choice for a first sewing project.

1

The Preliminaries

Before making up your mind to start sewing, stop and think about it seriously. Do you have the time to devote to it? Do you really want to concentrate this hard? Learning to sew will require about the same degree of attention that is needed for homework, general office work, or letter writing. Sewing is not a social activity—at least not until you can do it well. So don't expect to have friends in your home every time you plan to sew. Sewing is a do-it-yourself project.

Once you have made up your mind, choose a day or evening when you will be alone, when there is nothing you want to watch on TV, and when you don't have a good book to finish. Perhaps it's your husband's bowling night, or your boyfriend isn't coming to see you. Full-time homemakers should finish the housework and the meal planning. Students should finish studying.

In the beginning, you should allow at least two or three uninterrupted hours for sewing. Don't try to grab half-hours here and there during the day. And don't expect to finish your first garment the day you start it.

If you don't own a sewing machine, don't buy one right away. If you can borrow one, fine. If you do borrow one, however, make sure that you will have the time to use it and to return it by a specified date.

The Sewing Machine

If you can't borrow a machine, rent one. Some companies arrange for the rental fees to apply to the purchase price if you decide to buy the machine later. Since you might dislike the whole project and not want the machine, or you might find another one that you like better, leave yourself some options.

Rent only a good brand, such as *Singer, Kenmore* (Sears), *Necchi* or *Pfaff*. When you have learned how to operate the machine, you will know how to evaluate it. Then you can choose the one that is best for you. Properly cared for, a good machine will last a lifetime. As always, you get what you pay for.

You have to decide if you want a portable or console machine. There are advantages to both. If you have room, a console can double for another piece of furniture, a serving table or a lamp table, for example. A portable requires a strong table to set it on. A card table is generally not sturdy enough, but there are specially designed, easily stored tables for portables that add only a little to the cost. You can also use a breakfast or dining table. If these are too high for comfortable sewing, sit on a "booster" pad or cushion.

All good modern machines are excellent—amazing, in fact. You will be dazzled by the fascinating array of accessories, embroidery stitches, buttonhole makers, and bobbin-threading devices. The principal thing, however, is the ease of handling. Try the machine to see if it starts easily, smoothly, and *slowly*. For a beginner, this is important. You want to control the speed at all times, so get a machine which has a very slow, smooth take-off.

Most machines have a zigzag stitch—this is endlessly useful for many things. Chain stitching, which some machines can do, is useful for temporary seams and basting and can be ripped out easily. Most salesmen will demonstrate all the various features of their products, but you must not become bewildered; if you buy the machine later, you will receive a course of instructions in the use of the machine. Meanwhile, concentrate on the one thing you will need to know—does it start smoothly and slowly?

A Place to Work

You will need a good working space: a table for laying out the fabric and the pattern, for cutting, and for assembling. A dining-room table is perfect, and so is a drawing board. If neither of these is available, the floor is next best. Don't use a bed. The floor should be "hard" and unless the carpet is firm and smooth, it is not too good. Tape a couple of foam-rubber pads to your knees if you have to crawl around on the floor and make sure the area is clear and clean for a good distance around your working space.

Keep the ironing board and iron set up all the time you are sewing. There are a number of pressing aids you will want later, such as a tailor's gooseneck iron and a sleeve pad. When you consider how much you can save by making your own clothes, the cost of these refinements is negligible.

The Equipment

If you don't already have a sewing box, a shoe box will do very well for a start. In it you will have the basic tools: steel dressmaker's pins in two sizes, medium and fine; a magnet to pick them up with; needles in assorted sizes, some with large eyes; a tape measure marked on both sides; a pair of scissors with four- or five-inch blades; and a pair of scissors with one to one-and-one-half-inch blades for clipping and close work. Electric scissors are great, and you may want some later. Chalk and dressmaker's carbon paper are useful, and so is a stylus for the carbon paper. You should also have a thimble and a "ripper," which is a handy little gadget for breaking threads that is sold in notion departments.

You will buy thread to match the fabric you are sewing on, but you ought to have spools of white thread in 60 and 50 weights, and also black, for basting. Keep a supply of sewing machine needles in assorted sizes and some extra bobbins. Although a yardstick will hardly fit in the sewing box, it is a good thing to have around when you are sewing.

As you become more sophisticated, you will acquire more and more of the special tools that help produce professional-looking sewing. Some of these are described later, and you may discover others yourself.

Figure. 1. Your Sewing Box

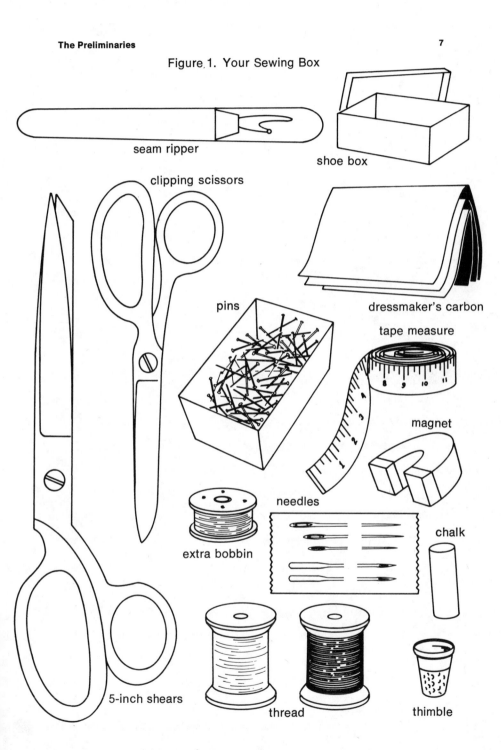

seam ripper

shoe box

clipping scissors

dressmaker's carbon

pins

tape measure

magnet

needles

extra bobbin

chalk

5-inch shears

thread

thimble

2

Clothes Talk

Irene made this blue, white, and beige
shift from an "Easy-to-Make" pattern.
She can use variations of this pattern
to make several other dresses.

2

Clothes Talk

The best wardrobe is a coordinated one, whether it is bought in the shops or made at home. The best-dressed women know this; they know what they look best in and they stick to it. They never buy clothes on whim. The entire wardrobe, whether it is bought all at once or over a longer period, is worked around a basic color scheme and a few becoming styles. Everything from a bikini to a ballgown is picked to conform to the colors that complement the person's eyes, hair, and skin tones, and the styles that flatter the figure.

Some of these well-dressed women wear the same colors all the time, year in, year out, summer and winter. They know what they look good in. Since there is practically no limit to the range of shades in any color, this need not be monotonous. Far from being monotonous, it creates a personal style or trademark, an identity. In an age when identity concerns us so much, when it is recognized as vital to self-realization, even this small contribution is worthwhile. This is not to suggest that clothes are all-important, but few women ignore appearance totally.

The single-color wardrobe has several advantages. The fact that everything "goes" together suggests that a smaller collection can actually function better than a large one. One coat can be worn with every outfit; a special handbag and shoes don't have to be bought for every dress; one skirt or pair of slacks can have many jackets and tops· accessories can be mixed and varied for any number of effects. And anything new will fit into the whole collection.

The Complete Wardrobe

The economy in fitting your wardrobe to one color scheme is almost too obvious to need pointing out. Compared to a closet full of clothes of every color, many of which are seldom or never worn, a small, well-coordinated wardrobe needs no defense. Clothes have a precarious life expectancy at best, considering the instability of fashion and the seasons. A small wardrobe costs less to begin with and produces a minimum "guilt-trip" in the event of a drastic fashion upheaval. Travelers know that a compact, versatile wardrobe can be composed of four or five basic costumes, and that the costumes are all the more satisfactory for being coordinated.

You need to make a number of preliminary decisions before actually planning a wardrobe. Just how do you want to look, for example? Do you have a life style which dictates the kind of clothes you can wear; or are you flexible, variable, interested in many activities, subject to many moods? Which are you?

Your appearance in general is pretty well established. It's true you can do things with your hair, with makeup, even with your figure if you are willing to work at weight control and posture, but in the end, you are you.

Clothes, on the other hand, are something else. If

you doubt it, remember dressing up in your mother's clothes as a child, or wearing a masquerade costume? Remember how different you felt, how different you *were?* Clothes can alter more than outward appearances. They can change moods, behavior, and attitudes. In an outfit that you know is becoming and appropriate, you can feel and act with self-confidence. But how do you feel in that dull, ill-fitting dress you wear when everything else is at the cleaners? You can feel one way in a floor-length skirt, another in a midi-length skirt, and still another way in a mini-skirt. You can stand out like a petunia in an onion patch in one dress and fade into a crowd without a trace in another. And enjoy both sensations.

A Style of Your Own

Over and above all of this, clothes can create impressions on other people. Clothes say things about you. However much truth there is in the old saying, "Clothes make the man," there is little doubt that many people believe it.

What do you want your clothes to say about you? You can make them say a great deal: that you have taste, imagination, flair; that you go your own way but don't ignore trends; that you interpret fashion with a personal twist; that you use fabrics with imagination; that you have made certain colors your own. All this adds up to one thing: you have created a "style" of your own.

You may not regard yourself as "artistic" or "creative" in the usual sense of these words, but sewing is an opportunity to express yourself in a field not considered unworthy by many very artistic and creative people. The selection of styles, the use of fabrics and colors, the workmanship—all these are components of a true craft. As a realizable form of self-expression and creativity, sewing can become a source of pleasure and satisfaction.

Study the Fashions

If you read the fashion magazines, you will find more than enough ideas for things you can make. As you study pattern books, you will find nearly every current fashion in one form or another. The chief thing is to *plan*.

Plan what? Since you can't start out making coats and suits, plan things that will go with the coats and suits you already have: blouses, shells, and tops for the suits; dresses and slacks that can be worn with the coats, or even with the jackets. Accessories are expensive. If you already have good shoes and handbags, plan things that will be good with them.

If, on the other hand, you are going to buy new accessories for the coming season, plan the clothes you are going to make around the new accessories. Get some samples of possible fabrics and see how shoes or bags look with them.

A summer wardrobe is comparatively inexpensive. The beginning seamstress has a chance to develop her skill with a modest investment; by fall, she is ready to tackle more difficult things and of course must spend more money for them.

So, let's start with spring. What should you make? How about a sleeveless shell, to wear with a suit from last summer? How about a pair of slacks to wear with sweaters you already own? Or an A-line dress to wear with shoes, bags, or scarves you still like?

None of these takes much time. Even the most timid person should not lack the confidence required to finish them. Having found that sewing is not as formidable a job as it appeared, the not-so-confident seamstress gains confidence.

Planning Ahead

For the determined, there is much more to do. You will have to plan ahead, you will have to know what you are going to need for the spring and summer. As you have read this book, you probably have already done some things. You have found out your favorite styles; you know what you wear best. You have analyzed your skin, hair, and eye colors and made tentative color schemes to match and complement these tones.

Now you must decide what you need: how many street dresses, how many slacks with tops, how many evening outfits. If you work, your wardrobe is quite different from that of a student, for example, or a girl who takes her baby to the park every day.

Let's design a hypothetical wardrobe for a girl with a part-time job, who spends some of her spare time swimming, playing tennis, and golfing, and who likes to entertain her friends with buffet suppers at home.

For work, she will want four or five dresses and one jacket that could make one or two of the dresses suitable for an evening on the town directly after work. This jacket would also have a skirt and slacks, making it work as two suits, together with three or four tops

or blouses. She would want two short tennis dresses
with matching shorts, a golf outfit and a swimsuit.
Something to wear over the swimsuit might be a full-
length terry robe, which would also serve as a bath-
robe. And, for at home, she would make a dashiki.

Her favorite color is blue, but because she tans well
in summer, she also likes white, beige, and cream.
Since this is a summer wardrobe, these light colors not
only look good in hot weather but can be found in a
wide selection of washable fabrics.

She starts with the jacket and skirt; a medium-
light beige linen. She selects a blue, beige, and white
printed linen for one sleeveless blouse; a dark beige
for another; a white cotton piqué with a waffle-weave
for a third. She makes two or three bright scarves in
several shades of blue, some with white, some with
other shades of beige, to wear with the blouses. Shoes
and bag are beige, similar to the shade of the jacket
and skirt.

The slacks to match the jacket can be worn with all
these blouses, of course, as well as with one or two
others. The blouses will also go with shorts of wash-
and-wear heavy cream cotton. One tennis dress is
cream cotton knit, with a darker beige stripe. The
other is white wash-and-wear cotton with matching
bloomers. Her swimsuit is bright blue double-knit synthetic in a tropical print of other blues and beiges and
splashes of vivid green. The white terry robe has a
hood and a rope belt.

Two of the dresses have been chosen to be worn
occasionally with the jacket. One is linen with an embroidered border of the same shade as the jacket; the
other is a blue-printed cotton with beige and white

designs that echo the beige of the jacket, with a collar and cuffs of the same linen as the jacket.

The other dresses are summery cotton prints, a blue, beige, white, and cream printed piqué, for example, and a beige and white checked gingham. Or, she could make a dress of blue wash-and-wear solid broadcloth, worn with one of the bright scarves. The only thing in the wardrobe not made at home is a tailored trench-coat-style raincoat that looks good for evening as well as daytime wear.

She lets herself go wild in the dashiki. It could be an African print in vivid electric blues with a black background, or she could select a tropical garden of exotic flowers in delicate blues, greens, and whites, with huge ferns, foliage, birds, and other fantasies. In any case, since it is worn with bare feet or sandals and loads of jewelry, the dashiki can either blend with the colors of her house or stand out sharply against a more neutral background.

Adding Up the Cost

How much should all this cost her? Taking a generous average of three yards per dress, at a cost of two to three dollars a yard, five dresses would cost around $37.50, plus not more than five dollars for the patterns. The linen suit, with skirt and slacks, would take about seven yards at around four dollars a yard, or $28, with two dollars for the patterns.

Two dollars a yard for the tennis dresses, and not more than two yards needed, would make them cost about four or five dollars apiece. A blouse without sleeves can be made from one yard of fabric—say the blouses might cost from two to five dollars each. The print for the dashiki could run from two dollars for a cotton print to six or eight for a synthetic or silk. Four or five yards of fabric would be required, so this could be the most expensive thing in the wardrobe. The terry-cloth robe would take four yards too, if it is full-length, at about three dollars a yard.

It might be interesting to make a swimsuit from the same print as the dashiki, and most swimsuits, especially bikinis, don't take much fabric, so the suit might cost only a couple of dollars more. Figure five dollars, to be safe. The whole wardrobe costs approximately $150 for eighteen garments, not including scarves and other accessories.

This wardrobe would be adequate for a whole summer vacation traveling or at home, for the average homemaker, or even for many working girls, with possible substitutions of fewer play-clothes and another dress or two.

The Business of Being Basic

The trick of this whole operation is the selection of basic patterns and a coordinated color scheme. Important choices are the styles of the dresses and the jacket; they have to suit each other. A box jacket without a collar is the safe choice for a beginner. An A-line or straight-line dress looks good with this jacket. For one version that can be worn with or without the jacket, a turtleneck collar or a band trimming can be used, if at first it is too difficult to make a regular collar.

Slacks with an elastic waistband are the easiest to make. In fact, they are the easiest to wear, too, because, with overblouses, slacks are flattering to nearly all figures. Slacks also lend themselves to endless variations with belts of matching and contrasting fabrics, leather, and other materials.

At least two of the dresses can be made from one pattern. Once you have found a pattern that suits you, there are many ways to use it—different kinds of fabric, different necklines, sleeveless, long, or short sleeves, different belts and scarves. The jacket, for example, can be made into a vest to be worn over blouses with long, full sleeves by omitting the sleeves. The jacket can be made into a full-length sleeveless coat, too, if an evening wrap is needed. This is especially elegant if the wrap is made in the same material as the long dress under it, but in another shade. Alternatively, the wrap could be a print worn over a plain fabric, or vice versa. One of the dresses you like in a short version can be made in a full-length version for evening, using a more luxurious material.

When patterns for the various garments have been selected, spend some time thinking about the kinds of *fabric* most suitable for each. Make notes. Cut out magazine pictures that show similar garments, to guide you when looking at materials. Above all, make up your mind about the *color scheme* you plan to use and stick to it. No matter how seductive those melting pinks look, if you decided on blue, buy blue. Next year, you might want to try a new color scheme and pink might fit, but the chances are that by next year you are going to know exactly what "your" color is and pink will not attract you.

To summarize the most important things about designing a wardrobe, remember the often-repeated axiom: *keep it simple.* Choose simple, basic styles, good quality materials, a consistent color scheme. Strive for good workmanship. Collect interesting accessories such as belts, scarves, sashes, beads, and other pieces of costume jewelry, and make them the focus of attention. Easily changed, they change the whole costume.

Develop a style of your own. Don't fight trends, don't be unfashionable, but take from current fashions the things that best become you, that contribute to your individual style and reinforce the image you want to maintain.

3

Patterns

Susan's maxi-dress, made from a very
simple pattern, gets its original look
from the bright orange and red cotton
fabric.

3

Patterns

Choosing your first pattern is not as difficult as choosing a husband. It's not as permanent a mistake if you choose unwisely, but a lot depends on the selection of your first sew-it-yourself garment. It's something like your first kiss—if you like it, you will try it again. And each time you try it, it gets better.

One thing will help a lot. Go over your present wardrobe and study the dresses you like the best, the ones you look best in. If you have a problem figure, be extra careful. In any case, be critical. Take *notes* on the exact features that make the dress good for you— neckline, sleeve length, belt placement. *Disregard* color. And prints. Other than for weight and drapability, disregard the fabric. If you happen to have a favorite dress, and it's in a Pucci print, ask yourself if it would still be your favorite in a plain color.

Think about cut, line, and fit—especially in simply styled dresses. Probably simple dresses are also your best dresses, but you have tended towards complicated styles. You may be in the habit of paying rather a lot for clothes. If you don't have any simple styles, however, go to the shops and try on some.

Try on the really simple things, which can be pretty expensive too, you will discover. Take note of the way effects are produced by scarves, belts, touches you could reproduce. But above all, concentrate on the lines and styles that look best on you.

Your Own Show

Right now, styles tend to be simple. T-shirt dresses, tank-tops, shifts, vests and "separates" are "in." Slacks are straight-hanging and unfitted. For this first venture into the unknown, you must select a simple style even if you have worn "fancy" things before. Because something is going to happen that didn't happen before; you are going to have complete control over this garment, you are going to plan it from beginning to end. The design, the fabric, the color, everything is up to you. Make it a smash.

The primary reason for making the garment simple, however, is to insure that you will really make it. If you don't finish your first dress, and wear it, you may never start another. You will have wasted the price of the pattern, the fabric, the machine—even this book. So save money: pick a simple pattern and promise yourself to finish the garment.

Looking at Patterns

All the pattern manufacturers have sections in their books marked *Simple to Make, Easy to Make* or *Jiffy*. Zero in on these. Don't pay any attention to the colors or prints shown in the books; concentrate on your notes. Don't pay attention to the hair styles or the faces or figures displaying the patterns—they are drawn all out of proportion and no matter what you look like, you won't look like them. Even when the designs are shown with photographs, remember that these are photographs of models, who usually weigh ninety-two pounds soaking wet. Trust your notes. If you did your homework, you will be able to select a pattern for a garment which will suit you.

Truly timid women who hate to take risks should consider making a caftan or a housecoat first, to get over the first qualms about the enormity of the undertaking. There's nothing wrong with this. If you pick a stunning fabric, it could become your favorite at-home garment. The compliments you get will inspire you to try something more daring. Or if you have a little girl, try making something for her. The rules still apply: *Keep it simple.*

When looking at patterns, study the books of several manufacturers. Make notes of more than one version of a similar style from different books. Ask to look at the patterns and for permission to remove the instruction-sheet from the envelope—without disturbing the pattern, of course.

See how many parts there are to the pattern and how the garment will be put together. I think the first thing that will strike you is how easy it all looks. And it will be, if you have concentrated on *Easy to Make* and *Jiffy* patterns, as recommended.

Read the back of the envelope. It will describe the garment, tell you how many yards of fabric are required in several widths, and list other items needed to complete the job. There may be a line reading, "Stripes, plaids and diagonal fabric not suitable." Do not ignore this.

There is usually another line or two listing several kinds of material which are suitable for this specific pattern. Don't ignore this either. Other important notations refer to "nap," "shading," "one-way design," or other qualifications, which have to be taken into consideration when estimating the required yardage. The salesperson in the yard goods will advise you about this when you buy the fabric.

Don't allow yourself to be rushed. Go back another day if you can't decide. Or buy one or two of the patterns you like best, with the agreement that they can be returned or exchanged if you wish. Most patterns are exchangeable if they are not unfolded; make sure before buying.

Don't allow yourself to be distracted. Stick to your notes. Don't go overboard for some enchanting outfit simply because it looks great in the book, if it does not conform to your plan. There is plenty of time later on for this kind of thing; right now you are just going to make a simple, easy-to-finish garment, and find out something about sewing in the process.

Just as with anything else, attitudes toward sewing can vary. If you feel like making sewing a big deal, it can get to be pretty much like work. If, on the other hand, you regard sewing as an art, a form of self-expression, it can become a source of great satisfaction. Apart from the value of the clothes you make, this value is even more lasting. Set a high standard for yourself in all the various steps of the process, for each step affects the one which follows it.

When you buy a pattern, consult the saleslady about your correct size. She will measure you and recommend the pattern size, which might not be the same as the ready-made dress you buy.

If your dimensions don't exactly match those of the recommended pattern, you can alter the pattern before cutting out the garment. Try to get at least one dimension, preferably the bust, to match your own. It is easy to adjust the waist or hip. Before attempting to alter the pattern, make sure you have your own accurate measurements to work with.

Altering the Pattern

Your work table should be clean and clear. Assemble the supplies—iron, ironing board, sewing box. To make alterations, you will need tissue paper, clear adhesive tape, a soft pencil, and a yardstick or ruler.

Press the pattern with a dry iron. *Don't* use steam on paper.

You'll notice that all the separate pieces of the pattern are for "half of" something—half the front or back, half a facing, one sleeve. This is because everything is cut double.

If you have bought the pattern size which is closest to your own measurements, you should not have to alter it more than one inch in any direction. All that is usually needed is a change in the length of the shoulder-to-waistline dimension, or an increase or decrease in the hip or bust.

If you need to alter the pattern to add one inch to the width of the whole garment, draw a line parallel to the cutting line, one-quarter inch outside the marked *Cutting Line* on the *Center Front* and *Center Back* of each piece of the pattern. There is usually enough excess paper for this, but if not, tape a strip of tissue paper to the pattern to allow you to draw this new line. Make sure you add to the facings and collar, if any. If the *Center Front* or *Center Back* are also marked *Place on Fold*, add the quarter-inch anyway. Now trim the pattern, cutting along the new lines you

Figure 2. Altering a Pattern

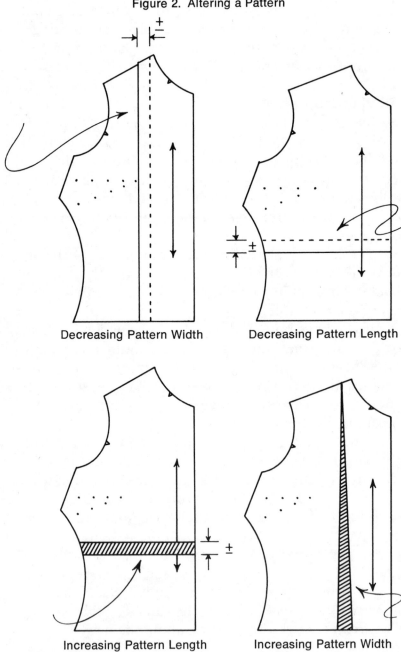

Decreasing Pattern Width   Decreasing Pattern Length

Increasing Pattern Length   Increasing Pattern Width

have drawn. Some patterns advise leaving the excess paper on and cutting through it as you cut the cloth, but cut it off at first because it will be easier.

If you want to increase only at the bust or hip and not all the way down the garment, *taper the line* you draw either down or up, as shown.

If the back or front of the pattern is composed of two segments, add one-eighth inch to *one side* of each of the two segments.

You can increase the pattern by cutting it apart, too. Draw a line parallel to the *Straight of the Goods* mark from the shoulder seam, near the neckline, to the waistline or hemline. Cut the pattern apart and tape a strip of tissue paper between the two pieces, adding *one-quarter* of the total required increase. This strip can be wedge-shaped if the increase is not needed throughout the entire garment.

If you need to decrease the pattern to take one inch out of the width of the entire garment, fold the front and back pieces of the pattern on a line parallel with the *Straight of the Goods* mark, from the shoulder seam to the hemline or waistline. Press on this line and make a one-quarter inch pleat on the line, taping the pleat down. The cutting line of the shoulder seam will have to be straightened. The straightening causes a slight decrease in the neck size, so the neck-facings and the collar must be lessened to match this decrease.

If the garment is to be made smaller at the bust but not at the waist, the pleat will be a wedge, tapering to nothing slightly above the waistline. If it is to be decreased at the hip but not at the bust, the wedge will taper to nothing slightly below the waistline.

Don't decrease or increase a pattern more than

three-eighths of an inch for any single piece of the pattern, or one and a half inches over-all. If your dimensions don't jibe with the dimensions on the pattern within one and one-half inches, you are buying the wrong pattern size.

Cutting

To prepare for cutting, first *press* the fabric. (See Chapter 4 for selection of the fabric.) If there is a *center fold*, make sure it is straight but don't press it. If the lengthwise edges—*selvages*—are not even, press out the fold and pin the material together again, along the selvage, making a new center fold. *Always* have the *right sides* of the fabric facing each other.

There is no right or wrong side to some materials. If you can't see the difference under a very strong light, there probably isn't any. Yarn-dyed cottons, for example, usually look the same on either side; prints are invariably one-sided.

Velvet and corduroy have *pile* or *nap* which is bent slightly in one direction. All parts of the pattern laid on a fabric with nap must run the *same way* so that when the garment is sewed together, the *rub* of the nap will always be in the same direction. If one sleeve, for example, has nap rubbing up and the other sleeve has nap rubbing down, they will look like two different materials when the dress is finished, much to your horror. Avoid this by laying the pattern out with all *tops* facing the same direction. Decide in advance which way you prefer the rub, up or down, in the finished dress.

Matching plaid is another source of disappointment, if you don't look ahead. There are two factors in plaid, the horizontal match and the vertical. Unfortunately, there are several tricky plaids which are not symmetrical, which adds another pitfall. However, with a bit of care you can outwit these traps.

Before starting to lay out the pattern on the fabric, open the material out and study the plaid. Decide upon one line in the plaid which will be the *center* of the front of the dress. Even if the dress is buttoned down the front, the *exact center* of the dress, where it laps, has to be centered on this one stripe. The pattern is always marked with *Center Front* even when this line is not on the fold of the goods.

Having selected a single line, see if the plaid is symmetrical on both sides of this line. If it isn't, as in some plaids, make sure that you have the strongest line in the plaid, even if all the lines on one side are not exactly in the same sequence as those on the other. If you can't decide on a line, use the *empty space* between sets of lines for the center.

Once you have selected center front, refold the material. Line up all the stripes both crosswise and lengthwise and pin them in place. You may have to pull and smooth to get them to match. Stick a pin through from the top and see that it comes in the same corner on the bottom layer before you are satisfied. This will take time. It is very much worthwhile, however, especially if you are sewing a wool plaid. On cotton it will be easier.

One of the fairly difficult plaid-matching jobs is with Thai silk. Because it is hand-loomed, it can be irregular. It helps to baste along one or two stripes, through both layers of the fabric, and press lightly. Pay less attention to vertical symmetry but take care to get a good *horizontal match*. Here again, all your extra efforts are worthwhile when you see how good a perfect match looks—heaven forbid that your first effort should result in a botched plaid-scramble!

When you have carefully matched the two layers of plaid together, you will have a "mirror match" on any two pieces cut from it.

When laying the pattern on the material, make sure to put the *Front* with its center line on the selected center line of the plaid. To achieve horizontal match, line up the *notches* on the side seams of both *Front* and *Back* on the same line in the plaid. There are usually two notches on side seams—make sure you line up the two top notches. In most cases, the horizontal match is the most noticeable so this is where you spend the most time to achieve a perfect result.

The instruction sheet enclosed with your pattern has several cutting diagrams; select the one which fits the width of material you are using and the version of the garment you are making. Encircle this diagram with a red crayon or marking pen.

Make sure the fabric is *straight* on the table; measure the edge parallel to the table if necessary. Be sure that there are no wrinkles on the bottom layer of fabric.

Place the pattern on the fabric in accordance with the diagram. Pin on the stitching line, being careful not to disturb the fabric or wrinkle it. Pin curves and corners rather closely, space straight lines further apart. The pins should be parallel to the cutting line.

Check to see that you have *all pieces* of the pattern pinned on the material before starting to cut. Read the instructions to make sure how many copies of each separate piece you need. If the fabric is thin, it is possible to make some parts double, for example, pockets; this means to cut four pockets instead of two.

Collars are always double; in a very thin fabric an interlining is used. The interfacing can be the same material, if the fabric isn't a print that would show through in a confusing way. Because of the various effects of washing or dry cleaning on fabrics, it is advisable to use the same material wherever possible in one garment. If interlining is advised on your pattern, consider this when cutting.

Use your long-blade scissors to cut out the garment. Don't disturb the cloth. Cut with the scissors flat against the table. If you find it hard to cut curves with the long scissors, use the short ones for these parts.

Leave the whole garment on the table and remove the scraps; save nothing smaller than six inches wide unless you have a long strip suitable for a belt. Don't throw away the scraps until the garment is finished— start a scrap bag then. Later you will find uses for large scraps to trim other garments or for interlining or even for a patch-work quilt. Patchwork skirts and vests are very attractive too.

Marking

Before removing the pattern from the fabric, mark where necessary. Along the edges you will find *notches*. Do not cut them out, but cut a *slash* about three-eighths to one-half inch deep in the seam-allowance. You will find *dots* marking the line of *darts*, sometimes at the back neckline, sometimes under the arms on the side seams. There are several ways to mark the darts. The material you are using will dictate the method.

In very heavy material with a close grain, you can mark with *carbon*. Place a piece of dressmaker's carbon paper, in a color which will show on your fabric, face up on the table under the place to be marked. Place another piece face down, under the pattern on top of the upper layer of fabric. Mark through the pattern, pressing the stylus hard enough to go through *both layers* of material. This will work for fairly heavy cloth and even for thin cloth if you are very careful to avoid moving the two layers while placing the carbon paper. Experiment first with a couple of scraps to see if you get a good visible mark.

When using carbon paper, don't remove all the pins from the pattern. Remove only those you have to take out to get the carbon paper in place. Cut the paper to a size that will slip under the pattern with a minimum of disturbance. Keep both layers of fabric exactly together, pinned if necessary.

For fabrics on which carbon paper won't work, marks can be made directly on the top layer of cloth with a *pencil* or *chalk*. A pin is then pushed through the pencil mark to the bottom layer of cloth and a mark made where the pin emerges. Naturally, the cloth is laid out with the right sides facing each other, so that marks will be on the *back* of the cloth.

When you are starting to sew, it may be easier for you to put the garment together if you mark the seam-allowance. This is tedious but pays off if you are not certain you can maintain an even margin when stitching. It will also help to keep the exact size of the garment, for even one-eighth of an inch off on four seams will result in a one-inch increase or decrease in the overall size of the garment. When you are more experienced, you will know exactly how much seam-allowance to take up on every seam, and marking will no longer be necessary.

If carbon paper or pencil marks will not show on the fabric you are using, make *tailor's tacks*. Thread a needle with a soft thread, 60 weight or finer, in a color that will show on the fabric. Make the thread a yard long and double it. Do not make a knot at the end. Take a *very small* stitch through the dot marking the dart and pull the thread through until a tail about four inches long is left. Take another very small stitch in the next dot, leaving a long *loop* between the stitches. Continue to take stitches until the thread runs out. Use as many long threads as you need to have a stitch

Figure 3. Marking Your Fabric

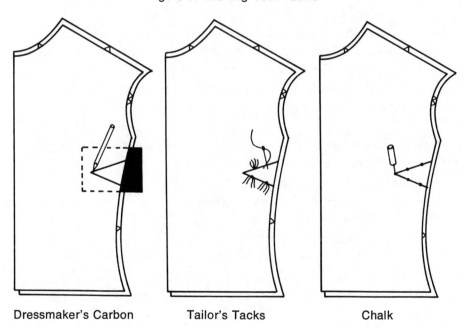

Dressmaker's Carbon   Tailor's Tacks   Chalk

in *every dot* marking the dart or any *other mark* required on your pattern. Make sure your small stitch goes through both layers of material.

When you are sure you have marked everything, cut the center of the loops between all the stitches and remove the pattern carefully. Now separate the two layers of material very slowly, pulling the separate stitches apart as you go. When the first stitch, nearest to the edge of the fabric, is about two inches apart, cut the threads between the *two layers* of fabric, leaving double pairs of thread on each layer of material. The bottom layer will have a tiny stitch showing on the wrong side with two double threads sticking out on the right side; the top layer of fabric will have double ends showing on both sides. Cut all the tailor's tacks apart carefully, making sure you don't pull the two layers of cloth too far apart as you go, for this will pull the tacks out of the top layer of fabric.

This may seem like a lot of work but it will repay you because when you are ready to sew, you can pin the separate pieces of the garment together with very little effort and with the assurance that you have matched them accurately.

If you do not mark seam-allowances on your pattern, trusting your ability to maintain an even margin when stitching, it will help to slash the two ends of the seams, so that when two pieces of the garment are pinned together, the two slashes for the seams will match. This will give you the right start for stitching.

A final word on marking. The time you spend marking is well spent; when the pattern has been removed, all those scraps of fabric don't look like much and the job of assembling them can seem formidable. If you have marked well, clearly indicating notches, darts, the position of pockets, buttons, and such, you will find following the instruction sheet much simpler than you had thought.

As important as marking is, care must still be used that the marks either be *easily removed* or *unseen* from the right side of the garment. For this reason, always try out the method of marking you are going to use to see how it works for your fabric. *Tailor's tacks* are absolutely safe; *chalk* is fairly safe but difficult to use for fine lines and dots; *pencil* is very good if it does not show, because it might not wash out; *carbon paper* is harder to handle and must be tried out to see how it washes. Experiment on your scraps before marking your garment.

4

Natural Fibers— Silk and Cotton

Angelo's dashiki is made of handwoven wool in black, white, and brown. Like all natural fibers, wool holds color well and can be woven into many textures.

4

Natural Fibers—Silk and Cotton

The selection of a material from which to make a dress involves a number of decisions. You may have some preferences already. Or you may know little or nothing about fabrics, how they are made, what they are good for, how they will stand up, and how to wash or clean them. You may be unaware of the limitless variety of beautiful materials available by the yard, from which you can fashion anything from a swimsuit to a wedding gown.

If you are only planning to make one garment at a time, that's one thing. If you are long-range planning, on the other hand, and want to create a balanced, versatile collection of clothes suitable for all occasions for several seasons, that's something else. In either case, you must know something about fabrics.

This chapter contains information on fiber content, weaves and designs, color and pattern, dyes and prints, and ways of evaluating fabrics for specific purposes.

Among the natural fibers from which dress goods are made are *silk, cotton, linen,* and *wool*—and blends of these, often mixed with animal fur or hair, such as vicuna, camel, and rabbit. Animal fur is most often mixed with wool to produce luxurious fabrics for coats and suits.

In one form or another, natural fibers have been used to make cloth since earliest recorded history, perhaps even earlier, for all we know. It is difficult for the chemists, no matter how skilled, to create fibers which rival, let alone surpass, the beauty of these natural materials. Natural fibers assimilate dyes readily, allowing the widest possible range of color. They can be woven into endless varieties of textures and patterns and in one way or another can meet every need for which textiles are required.

Many natural fibers are now processed to inhibit wrinkling, producing the *wash and wear* class of fabrics. These are often blends of natural fibers with synthetics. Again, the buyer is advised to ask for as much information as possible, to help preserve the beauty and durability of the fabric.

Silk: This fabric is generally associated with luxury, and indeed it is no wonder considering the colors, textures, and "feel" of the silks of Thailand, for example, or the brocades of France. However, there are silks, both imported and domestic, which are suitable for almost any use, from sport to formal attire.

Silk is expensive, generally, but for certain important things, indispensable. Most silks must be dry cleaned to retain body and color; those which can be washed require ironing. Almost no one will guarantee the washability, since no one can predict the treatment. However, it is easy to wash silk if you follow the rules: warm or cool water, mild soap made for washing fine garments; no harsh rubbing, no harsh wringing, no drying near heat. Each garment should be washed separately, with fresh water, rinsed two or three times, and rolled loosely in a towel for only long enough to absorb some of the water. Then it should be shaken out, gently pulled into shape, and finally hung, away from sunlight and heating elements, on a hanger which has been completely padded with a heavy towel.

A silk garment should be ironed before it is completely dry, with a warm iron, on the wrong side of the goods if possible. A steam iron which has a "silk" setting can be used, but the real trick is to take great care. Some silks lose some of their body when washed the first time; some of the stiffness is restored by ironing while the fabric is damp. Once more, experiment with scraps before washing and ironing your garment.

Because silk is so luxurious, it is desirable for dressy occasions. Even the simplest dress becomes a "costume" when made of Thai silk, silk shantung, or one of the many exquisite prints. Although you may not want to make your first garment of silk, you will be unable to resist forever the appeal of these fabrics. After you have gained experience and confidence, you will surely want a blouse or a dress of one of these beautiful textiles.

Sewing with Silk

Cutting and sewing silk is not harder than working with other materials. The weight of the fabric is the principal factor determining ease of handling. Thin materials—silk chiffon, nylon chiffon, cotton voile, synthetic sheers—are hard to manage. Very heavy fabrics are difficult for other reasons. So for your first few garments, stick to medium-weight materials with fairly firm weaves, regardless of fiber content.

Take care to keep the grain of the fabric straight

when laying out silk. Make sure the pins are sharp and don't leave holes where they will show. Use tailor's tacks for marking if chalk does not brush off readily. Take special care finishing raw edges, because some silks ravel easily. Use mercerized cotton thread for stitching, and avoid ripping because the needle holes might show.

Watch the temperature of the iron when pressing silk. Avoid pressing too much; silk looks best rather soft. When pressing seams open, press lightly and avoid knife-sharp edges, especially on hems and necklines. If the steam iron has a setting for "silk," make sure by experimenting on scraps that it will not alter the color or texture of the fabric. Some colors change with pressing but return to the original color when cool; make sure first.

When planning a dress of silk, make it from a pattern you have already used and know is good on you. Or make another dress first, of a less expensive material in the same weight and body as the silk, before starting the silk dress. This way you can tell if you are going to like it. There is nothing wrong with having more than one dress in the same design and you can avoid expense and disappointment. In any case, keep a silk dress simple. The fabric will "make" the dress.

Names of Silks

As you look at the silks in the dry goods department of your favorite store, you will note that silks come under several names. The following list gives a short description of some of them. The list also contains descriptions of terms used in the silk-garment industry:

Bengaline. Fabric woven of silk with horizontal ribs, similar to faille but heavier.

Broadcloth. Fabric woven of silk, very fine and smooth, slightly lustrous.

Brocade. Fabric woven of silk (or silk and metallic threads) on a jacquard loom, with all-over interwoven design in many colors and raised patterns; background may be satin-weave or twill-weave; comes in both lightweight and heavyweight versions.

Chiffon. Fabric woven of silk (or synthetic) in very thin, transparent plain-weave; used to describe other lightweight sheer fabrics, as chiffon velvet.

China Silk. Fabric woven of silk, originally in China, very soft and thin, almost transparent.

Crepe. Fabric woven of silk (and other fibers) characterized by a crinkled surface texture, obtained by weave or other means such as chemical action, embossing, or twisting yarns.

Crepe de Chine. Very sheer silk crepe, either slightly lustrous of raw silk, or shinier, with spun silk and "thrown" silk, the latter usually made in Japan.

Crepe, Faille. A fabric slightly heavier than crepe de chine, duller, smoother and richer looking.

Crepe Georgette. Fabric woven with two yarns of different twists, to produce a sheer, dull-textured surface, heavier than crepe de chine.

Crepe Matelasse. A double-woven fabric with a quilted appearance, very soft and drapable.

Crepe, Romaine or Rough. Semi-sheer or heavier crepe with rougher surface than faille.

Denier. Term indicating the size or number of a filament or yarn. As applied to silk, denier is determined by the number of .05 gram weights (deniers) of a standard skein of 450 meters. The higher the denier number the coarser the yarn.

Douppioni or *Duppion*. Silk fibers reeled from two silkworms in one cocoon together which produce a rough yarn used in shantung and pongee.

Faille. Fabric of silk woven with a crosswise rib and a crepe surface, slightly lustrous.

Hand. Refers to the "feel" of silk fabric and describes the texture and drapability.

Hand-loomed. Silks made on hand- or foot-powered looms using irregular yarns and having interesting textures and colors.

Honan. Highest quality Chinese (Taiwan) silk, usually woven with blue selvage.

Iridescent Fabrics. Silks woven with one color on the warp threads, another on the filling or weft threads, producing a changeable color.

Lamé. Fabric woven of silk and metallic threads to produce a rich pattern, using the metallic thread for the design (as in Sari silks), or using metallic thread as background with silk threads making the designs.

Moiré. A finish on silk fabrics which gives a wavy or watered effect on the surface. The effect is produced by crushing some of the parts of the fabric in one direction and others in the opposite direction, to reflect light and change the apparent color.

Nub Yarn or *Slub Yarn*. Yarn with several thicknesses throughout its length, some heavy and twisted "nubs" alternating with finer segments; when woven into cloth, the texture is irregular as in pongee and shantung.

Panné Satin. Fabric of silk with a satin finish, but of much higher luster than ordinary satin.

Panné Velvet. Fabric of silk, woven in a cut pile texture, but with the pile pressed flat in one direction; very lustrous and lightweight (also made in synthetic fibers).

Peau de Soie. Fabric of silk with a satin texture on both sides, slightly ribbed, slightly stiff, very luxurious.

Pure Silk or *Pure Dye Silk.* Silk fabrics which do not contain more than 10 percent by weight of finishing materials, such as metallic weighting.

Raw Silk. Fabrics woven from silk yarns in their natural state, such as pongee.

Romaine. Silk fabric with a texture similar to crepe, semi-sheer, heavier than Crepe Georgette.

Satin. A fabric woven in silk, with a satin-weave and a lustrous finish produced by running the fabric between hot cylinders; comes in various weights and degrees of shininess.

Shantung. A fabric woven with a nubby surface, usually from wild-silk yarn, similar in texture to pongee. Shantung comes in all colors; it is very luxurious. Thai or Thailand silks are outstanding examples, woven with various colors into checks, plaids, stripes, and solids.

Silk. Natural fiber from the cocoon of the silkworm, originally developed in China, which comes either white or yellow after the gum is removed. Wild silkworms produce a darker tan fiber. "Silk" also refers to any fabric woven from silk fibers entirely. Silk fibers and silk materials have natural resilience and resist wrinkling.

Surah. Soft, twill-weave fabric of silk, often woven in plaids.

Taffeta. Fabric of plain-weave silk with slight sheen,

stiff texture and fine pebble finish, often woven
with two colors interlaced to produce iridescent
or changeable effect; comes in various classifica-
tions, such as Antique Taffeta (made with nubby
yarn to produce a rough texture), Faille Taffeta
(with a crosswise rib), Moiré Taffeta (with a wa-
ter-silk effect), Paper Taffeta (very light with a
paperlike finish), and Tissue Taffeta (very thin
transparent taffeta).

Thai Silk. A type of shantung or pongee fabric made
in Thailand, of medium heavyweight and made in
exceptionally delicate and rich colors, woven in
stripes, checks, and plaids in interesting combinations; very luxurious.

Tricot. A fabric knitted from silk fibers in single- or
double-bar construction, usually in prints for
dress goods, plain for lingerie.

Velvet. Fabric woven of silk (or silk with another
fiber, usually cotton), woven with a short, soft
thick warp pile surface, usually cut; comes in several variations, such as Bagheera (with an uncut,
crepelike pile), Chiffon Velvet (very soft and
thin), Cisele Velvet (with a pattern of cut and uncut pile), Lyons Velvet (very stiff and thick),
Nacre Velvet (with the back of one color and the
pile of another to produce a changeable effect),
and Transparent Velvet (very thin, light in weight
and soft).

Yarn-Dyed Silk. Fabric made of silk fibers which are
dyed before they are woven or knitted into cloth.

Sewing with Cotton

Cotton may be the most versatile of all natural

fibers. It can be spun and woven into fabrics as heavy as canvas, strong enough to cover a truck; or into fabrics thin as spider webs, light enough for a baby's christening gown. Between these two extremes are thousands of weights, weaves, patterns, and textures —in thousands of colors.

Only a small part of this great cotton selection will be described here, for as you increase in skill, you will investigate all kinds of fabrics, including cotton. Experience and personal preference will do the rest.

Piqué is easy to handle and looks crisp and tailored when finished, and therefore it's an excellent first choice for "good" dresses. Since it requires no special handling, will hold its shape during the sewing processes, and will stand up under fairly adverse treatment, it's a natural for the beginner. Piqué comes in ribs, small and large, and many raised shapes, geometric and floral. The quilted or "waffle" effect results in a firm fabric very resistant to wrinkling which looks cool even in the hottest weather. It is suitable for a wide range of uses, from formal party dresses to playsuits.

Sailcloth refers to a number of medium and heavyweight, closely woven fabrics similar to *canvas*. While canvas itself is not readily available in dress-goods stores, it has interesting possibilities if you can locate it.

The natural color of canvas is a warm cream or off-white and the finish is uneven, crisp, and slightly rough. It must be preshrunk, because it could shrink up to 15 percent with the first washing. Even allowing for shrinkage, it's really very inexpensive. It can be used straight from the dryer, with only a little pressing, for sports clothes with a nautical air. With a spray-

on water-repellent finish, canvas could make a great
raincoat. When you are ready to make slipcovers, canvas is perfect for durable, washable, attractive furniture covering.

Regular *sailcloth* looks something like canvas, but
it's lighter in weight, more even in texture and does not
shrink so much. It comes in many solid colors and
prints, some *permanent press*. The edges of all printed
materials show wear first; on sailcloth this makes
lengthening hems on children's clothes impossible
after repeated washing.

Gingham refers to a wide variety of medium and
lightweight fabrics, usually yarn-died and therefore
color-fast. Gingham is a preferred material for children's clothes because of its durability, washability,
and good looks. However, its use is by no means lim-
ited to children's things. Indeed, its variety and reasonable cost make it the ideal choice for the beginning
seamstress. It makes delightful summer dresses, even
evening dresses. Your first venture could be a full
maxi-length dance dress in blue checked gingham—
two different sized checks, even two different colors—
or a mini-dress in one check with its own coat in another check. Or, choose a stripe. Or any combination
of colors or weaves. Or a see-through dashiki for
around the house, to wear with a bikini, in a multi-
striped crisp gingham. Just looking at the variety of
designs available in this versatile fabric will give you
plenty of ideas.

Organdy and *Voile* are thin cotton fabrics, the first
very stiff and crisp, the second soft and clinging. Collars and cuffs of white organdy are used on many simple dresses of other fabrics, both cotton and wool, for
a demure and youthful effect. Some of the more so-

phisticated couturiers have used these seemingly simple fabrics for spectacular effects involving ruffles and layers of various colors—when you are ready to tackle a costume of this kind, don't forget organdy. Voile is hard to work on, just as most thin material is.

The kind of garment you are making always dictates the kind of fabric; if you want a soft, clinging and floating kind of dress, there are hundreds of different weaves that are easy to use. The principal thing to think about is how well the material will hold its shape while you work. Look at a single layer of the cloth and visualize the process of stitching a number of separate pieces together. Thin materials make good gathered skirts, for example, but they don't look particularly good in straight, tight fitting, unlined dresses. Long full sleeves, long full skirts, and ruffles are perfect for thin material; if this is your style, learn to master thin materials from the beginning.

Thin materials, of cotton and all other fibers, take more time. It is necessary to cut, baste and stitch with extra patience and care, to avoid losing the shape of the individual parts of the garment. The machine will sometimes pucker the cloth instead of stitching it smoothly. To avoid puckering, baste a strip of tissue paper on top of the seam to be stitched. Let the needle go through the paper first and tear off the tissue paper after you finish. Most very thin, transparent fabrics like cotton voile and silk or nylon chiffon require French seaming or bound seams. (See Chapter 9.) Nevertheless, beautiful garments are made from some of these confections, and sooner or later you will want to try your hand. Make sure you are using the finest grade *needle*, that all the settings, both *stitch tension* and *bobbin tension*, are correct. Use 60 or 70 grade thread, unless you are *shirring*, where the next heavier grade can be used if it will not pucker. Most important of all, select a pattern appropriate for the fabric. Since you are going to put in some extra effort, make sure it will be rewarded. Appropriateness, of course, applies to all fabrics; nothing is more important than that pattern and fabric be suited to each other. If you have any doubts, refer to the suggestions on the pattern envelope and consult the salesperson.

Cottons of all weights come in some of the most delightful prints imaginable, ranging from tiny dots and flowers to over-scaled geometrics and abstracts. Your own taste in these matters should lead you. One word of warning, however. Scale is so important that it is hard to over-emphasize it. Large prints can increase your over-all size. Small prints can do the same thing, however, by contrast. In general, the use of the garment is a good guide; for casual clothes, for sports and at-home or entertaining clothes, prints in extreme color combinations and large designs work very well. For business, street clothes, and public appearances, more conservative colors and designs are in good taste, unless you really want to call attention to yourself.

What is appropriate on a teen-ager or young girl is not always suitable for someone older. This applies to the selection of prints and colors as well as to the selection of patterns. It is very easy to be carried away with fabrics by-the-yard, and to forget to visualize how they will look when made up into a dress. If you have doubts about anything, look at ready-made clothes in similar prints and fabrics and see if you still want, say, that tropical garden in purple and green.

But everyone should let themselves go once in a while, so do have a wonderful wild print in some kind of garment, if only a blouse to wear with a plain suit, or a housecoat for Sunday morning breakfast. It will give you a lift, and your family a lift, too. For these garments, cotton prints are absolutely ideal. They cost little, they are easy to sew, and they launder well. If you begin your sewing career with cotton prints, stripes, checks, solids, chances are you will continue to sew until you become a real "pro."

Don't overlook the exciting native or African prints now available nearly everywhere. These are very good if you are making a shirt for a man or any of the kaftan or dashiki-type garments. Experiment before laundering for the right care, because some of these brilliantly colored textiles run or fade.

Many cotton fabrics are labeled *Care-Free, Wash and Wear,* or *Permanent Press.* Obviously this is an advantage for children's clothing, sportswear, and anything which is laundered often. However, special care should be given to "good" dresses and suits whether or not they are so labeled. Even *wash and wear* garments repay a little extra trouble.

Wash a "good" cotton dress separately in moderately hot water, with mild soap. Rinse thoroughly. Use moderate heat in the dryer or air-dry on a well-padded hanger, away from direct sunlight or heating elements. Press damp, on the wrong side first if possible; use spray starch sparingly if a little stiffness is desirable.

For the rest of the laundry, separate all the *wash and wear* things and handle them the same way you would handle the "good" garment alone. Very high temperatures are not good for any treated fabrics.

Names of Cottons

Cotton fabrics have special names, the same as

silks do. Here are a few of them, along with terms
used in the cotton-garment industry:

Basket Weave. A type of fabric woven with two or
more warp and weft threads woven side by side to
resemble a plaited basket.

Batiste. Sheer cotton fabric, woven of fine combed
yarns, with a mercerized finish.

Broadcloth. Plain, tightly woven, lustrous cotton
cloth with fine crosswise rib, similar to poplin but
finer. Made of finest quality pima or Egyptian cotton fibers. (Also made of wool.)

Calico. Plain woven, printed cloth, similar to percale,
of cotton fibers.

Cambric. Soft woven cotton fabric treated with slight
glaze, used for costumes; not washable.

Canvas. Heavy, firm cotton fabric used for needle-
work, awnings, interfacings.

Chambray. A plain woven fabric with white warp and
colored weft, which has a slightly mottled appearance.

Chintz. Glazed cotton fabric usually printed with flowers and bright colors. Some chintzes have permanent glaze, suitable for wearing apparel.

Colorfast. Will not fade or change color noticeably.

Combed Yarn. Cotton yarn spun from cotton which
has been combed to remove short fibers, producing more uniform weaving.

Corduroy. Cotton cut-pile fabric with wide or narrow
wale.

Cotton. Soft fiber obtained from seed pod of cotton
plant, of different fiber lengths. Long fibers found
in such types as pima, Egyptian, and Sea Island
are the best quality.

Count of cloth. Number of threads per inch; lengthwise (warp) yarns also called "ends"; crosswise or filling yarns also called "picks." Example: broadcloth shirting: 144 x 76.

Crepe. Lightweight fabric of cotton (or silk, wool, or synthetic) with a crinkled surface. The surface effect of crinkling is called plissé.

Cretonne. Cotton fabric, similar to chintz, without glaze.

Denim. Twill-weave cotton fabric made with white filling yarn and colored warp yarn.

Dimity. Sheer cotton fabric with a corded stripe or checked weave.

Dotted Swiss. Rather stiff sheer cotton fabric woven with dots or spots, from Switzerland (or the United States).

Drill. Strong cotton fabric similar to denim with diagonal weave; twill.

Duck. Tightly woven cotton fabric similar to canvas.

Finish. Treatment given by hot-roller process to fabrics to produce certain surface effects, such as embossing or glazing. Special finishes can be applied to make a fabric water-repellent, wrinkle-resistant, or able to retain pleating. Finish can give dull or shiny surface and can give "feel" to fabric.

Gabardine. Cotton version of heavy, tightly woven twilled fabric with diagonal fine rib.

Gingham. Yarn-dyed, plain-weave fabric of cotton, woven in medium weights in stripes, checks, and plaids.

Glazing. Treatment given to cotton fabric with hot roller and starch, glue, paraffin, resin, or shellac to produce a polished surface. Some glazing processes can be made permanent.

Herringbone Twill. Chevron weave, a broken twill cotton weave alternating the direction of the diagonal rib.

Homespun. Similar to fabric made of yarn spun at home; rough textured of uneven fibers.

Hopsacking. Basket-weave cotton similar to burlap.

India Print. Somewhat coarse cotton fabric hand-block-printed with traditional India designs; usually made up into squares or the size of bedspreads.

Lawn. Light thin cotton material.

Madras. Finely-woven cotton fabric in striped, checked, and plaid effects, in various colors, usually intended to fade to softer blends.

Mercerizing. Treatment for cottons using caustic soda which makes the fibers stronger, more lustrous, and more easily dyed.

Monk's Cloth. Heavy, basket-weave cotton similar to hopsacking and burlap.

Muslin. A basic cotton fabric, in firm plain-weave, ranging from thin batiste to heavy sheeting.

Ninon. Voile; smooth, finely-woven transparent cotton fabric.

Organdy. A thin, transparent, stiff cotton fabric usually treated to retain its crisp finish; may have a self-colored shadow pattern.

Oxford. Shirt-weight cotton fabric with slight basket weave.

Percale. Medium-weight, firm, plain-weave cotton fabric with smooth surface, usually in a solid color.

Piqué. Cotton fabric with cord, waffle, or other design woven in, sometimes similar to quilting.

Poplin. Plain-weave cotton fabric similar to broadcloth with slightly heavier rib.

Sailcloth. Strong, firmly woven cotton fabric similar
to canvas or duck.

Sanforizing. Trade name for process to reduce shrinking of cotton fabrics.

Sateen. Cotton fabric with sheen surface, used for lining; cotton satin.

Seersucker. Lightweight cotton fabric woven with
alternating crinkled stripes which are held in
permanent position by firm stripes; requires no
ironing.

Selvage. The reinforced lengthwise edge of the cloth.

Structural Design. A woven-in design as opposed to
one printed on a fabric.

Terry. Cotton fabric with loops forming pile on one
or both sides; water-absorbent, used for towels
and beach robes.

Twill. Basic weave, with distinct diagonal rib woven
in; denim, drill, and gabardine are twill weaves.

Velvet. Cotton fabric made with an extra set of warp
threads which are cut to produce a thick "pile"
like fur, usually about one-eighth inch or less.

Velveteen. Cotton fabric, similar to velvet, with
shorter pile, cut from filling threads instead of
warp threads, not quite as soft as velvet.

Voile. Fabric of plain-weave, very soft, sheer, and fine;
similar to organdy, but not stiff; sometimes
printed.

Wale. The ridge or rib in a cotton fabric; sometimes of
pile, as in corduroy.

Warp. Yarns running crosswise in woven cloth;
"ends."

Washable. Fabrics which will not run, fade, or shrink when washed in soap and water.

Wash-and-wear. Fabric which does not require ironing after washing in soap and water.

Weave. Process of forming cloth by interlacing threads running crosswise (filling, "picks," or weft threads) with threads running lengthwise (warp, "ends") either by hand-operated looms or machine looms.

Plain-weave, Twill-weave, or *Satin-weave.* Looms are plain or jacquard; jacquard looms can pick up certain sets of thread to produce intricate designs with changing colors.

Yarn. The fiber produced from spinning cotton, silk, wool, linen, or synthetic; a continuous strand used for weaving or knitting; thread is composed of several yarns twisted together for strength, for sewing.

Yarn Dyed. Yarns dyed before being woven or knitted into fabric.

5

Linen, Wool, Synthetics

The author wears a basic dress of beige linen. Linen, one of the world's most elegant fabrics, is also one of the easiest fabrics to sew.

5

Linen, Wool, Synthetics

Couturiers, dress manufacturers, and expert home seamstresses all regard linen as an aristocrat worthy of their best efforts in design and workmanship. You will too, when you make your first garment of this elegant and versatile fabric. Linen tailors well; that is, it can be cut and sewed to produce crisp, clean-cut clothes that hold their shape and color for the life of the garment.

Linen comes in several weights suitable for dresses, suits, and slacks. A lightweight grade called "handkerchief" linen is used for blouses, baby clothes, and even formal gowns. Because of its durability and stability, it is ideal for hand-embroidering and is the first choice for those who wish to embellish a garment with a colorful border or monogram. The simplest dress becomes special, in linen, with embroidered decorations. Many linens come machine-embroidered, with overall patterns or borders of various widths.

Printed linens are among the most attractive of the printed textiles and suggest possibilities for combinations of solids and prints, suits with matching and contrasting blouses, all sorts of costume-making inspirations. Most linens are treated with a permanent-press process which eliminates the tendency to wrinkle.

Sewing with Linen

Linen is one of the easiest fabrics to sew. It holds its shape admirably, can be easily cut and handled, needs no special treatment in stitching, and presses perfectly. Raw edges should be zigzagged or overcast, but raveling is not excessive. The typical "slubbed" weave is produced by the irregularity of the fibers and is responsible for the rich texture of the cloth.

Linen lends itself to "good" clothes perfectly, but is not out of place for casual or sportswear. With reasonable care on your part, you can produce a truly professional-looking garment even the first time out, with linen. As in the case of silk, a simple pattern and fine workmanship can allow the beauty of the fabric to "make" the garment.

Linen washes well. It must be ironed but will look good if given some care. If the garment is lined, dry-cleaning might be advisable. If you intend to wash a lined linen dress, pre-shrink both linen and lining before cutting either. This of course applies to any lined garment you intend to wash. Always wash a linen dress alone, in moderately hot water with mild soap, and moderate heat in the dryer. Press damp, on the wrong side first.

Names of Linens

These are some things to know about linens:

Bundle Linen. Coarse Irish linen, handmade in twenty-four-inch widths.
Bleaching. Process for removing natural impurities

from linen yarn or cloth to produce pure white goods that can accept dye or printing; improves fabric's ability to absorb dye; bleaching may be done with chemicals or by exposure to sunlight, air, and moisture.

Butcher Linen. Linen fabric similar to crash.

Crash. Coarse fabric of linen, woven from rough, irregular yarns of various thicknesses to produce an uneven surface.

Flax. Fibers of the flax plant which are spun into linen yarns.

Handkerchief Linen. Sheer, lightweight plain-weave linen.

Hand-loomed. Hand-woven fabrics of linen which are woven on hand- or foot-powered looms.

Hand-spun. Linen yarns spun by hand.

Homespun. Fabric spun and loomed by hand; fabric manufactured to resemble the rough, uneven texture of real homespun fabrics.

Irish Linen. Fine grade, medium weight or lightweight linen, usually made by hand, from Ireland.

Linen. Strong, lustrous yarn or fabric woven of flax fibers; woven plain or jacquard fabric in various weights.

Moygashel. Trade name for fine quality Irish linen.

Spun Linen. Finest grade hand-woven linen.

Sewing with Wool

The variety in woolen textiles is probably greater than in any other single group of materials. Woolens include all the heavy coat fabrics, the medium and lightweight coatings, numerous weights for suits, and a limitless choice of weights for dresses. Strands of many kinds of yarns of many thicknesses are mixed, blended, crimped, twisted, looped, and fringed to create loose weaves and tight weaves, smooth finishes and rough ones. There seems to be no end to the ingenuity of designers of wools, and no end to the number of fibers they can create with.

But don't be intimidated by wool. Because expensive suits, winter coats, and tailored clothes in general are nearly always made of wool, a beginner may think it's too hard to handle. While it's certainly true that you can't start out making a tailored garment, there are still plenty of simple wool skirts, jumpers, and even dresses that are within your capabilities. If you learn to sew well, you will sooner or later decide to tackle tailoring, and at that time you may want to take lessons in this special branch of the art of sewing. Meanwhile, concentrate upon the many easy things which can be done with wool.

Considering only those wool fabrics suitable for dresses, slacks, and skirts, there is still an enormous range of choice. There are sheers almost as fine as silk, many kinds of knits, textured tweeds, smooth flannels, and ribbed gabardines. Although there are some printed woolens, the usual method of creating pattern or design in wool is to incorporate the design elements into the weaving process itself. For example, yarns of various colors are used both crosswise and lengthwise in plaid, to create other colors where they cross each other. With complex weaving techniques, all sorts of designs can be produced with yarns of different colors, weights, and textures.

Flannel is a popular wool fabric which can be made into skirts or jumpers by a beginning seamstress. Although flannel comes in various weights, the lighter ones are best for you. One way to determine when a fabric is going to be too heavy for you to sew success-fully is to hold a double thickness of the material be-tween two fingers. This is a seam and its seam-allowance, and if the doubled fabric folds flat and retains its flexibility, it ought to be fairly easy to handle.

The heavier a fabric is, the greater difficulty you will have when turning back the seam allowance on places like the neckline or the armhole. For this rea-son, start your first wool dress from a pattern which does not have a collar to avoid a seam around the neck that contains several thicknesses of material. The bodice will have two thicknesses of goods for the col-lar (at the ends of the collar it will be four thicknesses because of the seam joining top and bottom collar) and the facing, plus the seam allowance for both bodice and facing. As you can see, this adds up to eight layers of material—if it is a heavy fabric, that's a lot of wool. When you encounter this multiplication of layers in thinner goods, you naturally trim off the var-ious seam-allowances to get a smooth appearance. You can do the same with wool, but it is more difficult because of the extra weight. This is one of the prob-lems of tailoring, which we are not dealing with here.

So, look at *thin woolens* and choose patterns with very few seams: skirts without waistbands, for exam-ple; or jumpers without sleeves or collars. And when-ever possible, face woolen garments with a good grade of silk or synthetic in a matching color to reduce the thickness of the neckline and armhole seams. If, for example, you choose a navy blue textured wool for a jumper, face it with navy blue crepe or a navy and white small dot, pattern, or stripe, and make a blouse of the same material. Make a scarf, too, to wear with the jumper and a plain white blouse.

Lightweight wools, suitable for the beginner, include *flannel, gabardine, sheer crepes, tweeds*, and especially *knits*. Knits come in many weights, in plain colors and in stripes. The newer knits come in various interesting patterns.

If you are careful to select an appropriate pattern for a wool dress, you should be able to sew one of the light jerseys as easily as a synthetic of comparable weight. My personal preference being for natural fibers, I would recommend wool because the finished garment will retain its shape, will repay ordinary good care in dry cleaning with many seasons of wear, and will look much more expensive than it actually is.

Wool is not more difficult to cut than any other fabric, except that the edges of *loose weaves* must be finished immediately to prevent raveling. The difference in sewing has been suggested above; many layers of heavy fabric result in lumpy seams.

Wool knits, like all knits, require a special stitching technique. The fabric must be gently stretched with both hands as it runs under the sewing-machine needle. If the fabric is stretched too much, it will not return to normal; too little stretch will result in strain on the stitching during wear. Even on ready-made clothes the seams can rip out with wear, of course. Don't add to this problem by making anything too tight. Use a moderately small stitch but make sure the fabric returns to normal size after stitching. If the fabric stays stretched when you are no longer holding it, the stitch may be too small. Steam the seam as soon as you finish it and you will be able to tell if it's right.

One disadvantage of all knits is seat-sag. To help

obviate this, line all skirts. Use lining material with a very firm, smooth surface which does not stretch at all, and make the lining slightly smaller than the skirt. Press knit garments, at least in the back of the skirt, as often as they are worn, steaming out the sag.

Repeated wear sometimes produces shine on wool material, especially in the seat. Dry cleaning can remove it for a long time, but ultimately everything wears out. Sponging lightly with vinegar is said to help, but testing on a scrap is advised here as always, to see what happens to the color and finish of the fabric.

Slacks are not hard to make, if you use a pattern with no waistband or zipper, but an elastic waistband. Slacks are best made in knits and should fit fairly snug, that is, they should pull up over the hips but not have excess material around the hips once they are in place. If you are inclined to be overweight, this is surely the most becoming kind of pants you could wear. A good pair of wool knit slacks with a matching or related jerkin or vest can be a good beginning for your sewing career.

Unlike other wool fabrics, jersey or knit woolens do not require facing of other fabrics unless they are exceptionally heavy. The edges of knits do not ravel easily and seams can be pressed flat to produce a smooth unbroken surface. Avoid trimming seam-allowance too close in case a seam rips, because you will want to re-stitch it and it is very hard to stitch close to the cut edge. If you use the special thread developed for knits, remember how it reacts to heat.

Names of Wools

Woolen fabrics are found with the following

names; other terms that are found in the wool-garment
industry are also listed:

Alpaca. Long fine hair of South American animal used
   in combination with wool for fabrics of great
   warmth and softness, for coats; combined with
   other fibers for other types of cloth.

Angora. Long fine fibers of goat hair, used in combination with wool and other fibers to make cloth; Angora rabbit hairs, used the same.

Australian Wool. Wool derived from sheep of Spanish
   Merino stock, raised in Australia; strong, long
   staple, soft and elastic.

Bengaline. Fabric of wool (or wool and other fibers)
   woven with a crosswise cord or rib, similar to
   faille.

Bouclé. Fabric woven of wool (or wool and other
   fibers) with a crinkled or knotted yarn, to produce a rough texture; sometimes knitted.

Broadcloth. Smooth, rich-looking woolen fabric with
   twill back and slightly napped face, with velvety
   feel; there are also broadcloths made of cotton,
   silks, and blends.

Camel Hair. Fibers of camel hair combined with wool
   to make fine, soft fabric so-named; also yarn for
   knitting using camel hair.

Caracul Cloth. Heavy woolen fabric made with nap
   of curled and twisted loops; astrakhan cloth.

Cashmere. Fabrics made from the soft wool of the
   Indian Kashmir goat, or similar domestic goats;
   usually combined with wool for fabrics of more
   durable finish.

Challis. A pure-wool fabric of fine wool yarns, very

thin and soft, usually printed with small floral design; now made in blends and synthetics.

Cheviot. Wool fabric named for Cheviot Hills in England; similar to serge, with slightly rough surface, often of worsted yarn.

Chevron Weave (Herringbone). Wool fabric woven in twill-weave zigzag or broken pattern.

Chinchilla Cloth. Heavy twill-weave wool fabric with tufted or nubby napped surface.

Covert. Diagonal twill-weave fabric of wool with smooth, impervious finish, sometimes water-repellent or treated with water-repellent chemicals.

Donegal. A homespun or homespun-type of rough tweed made from irregular thicknesses of wool with slubs or spots prominent in the surface.

Felt. Wool fabric made up of fibers which are not knitted or woven, but are manufactured with moisture, heat, chemical action, and pressure, which produces a perfectly smooth, flexible, and textureless material.

Flannel. A soft-nap, wool fabric, generally light in weight with great flexibility, good draping qualities, and a smooth, somewhat lustrous finish.

Gabardine. Tightly woven wool fabric with a strong diagonal twill rib.

Hand-spun. Wool yarn spun by hand, slightly irregular.

Hand-loomed. Wool fabric woven on hand- or foot-powered loom; hand-woven.

Harris Tweed. Wool tweed spun, dyed and hand-woven in the Hebrides.

Heather Mixture. Wool fabric, usually tweed, woven

of yarns in mixed colors suggesting the colors of the heather plants and flowers.

Homespun. Wool fabric made by hand in the home, or made to copy the rough, uneven appearance of these.

Kasha. Wool fabric made of natural fibers from goats of Tibet, slightly streaked because of the variations in natural colors.

Kashmir. Cashmere.

Keratin. Protein substance, the chief component of wool fibers.

Llama. Fibers from the underfleece of the South American llama, similar to camel's hair, usually combined with wool to make fine fabrics.

Melton. Thick, heavy wool fabric with a felt-like appearance.

Merino. Fibers from merino sheep which are woven into very fine, soft fabrics or knits.

Mohair. Fibers from Angora goats, usually combined with other wool fibers for fabrics; fabric with stiff pile of wool and mohair.

Serge. Twill-weave fabric of wool with diagonal rib on both sides.

Sharkskin. Twill-weave fabric of wool in two colors, resulting in a small check or nail-head effect.

Tartan. Any of a group of wool plaids in the designs of the Scotch clans.

Tropical Worsted. Lightweight fabric for summer clothing, made of wool, or wool and other fibers, in various weaves.

Tweed. A wool fabric woven, originally by hand, of yarns dyed before weaving, in irregular threads to give a rough surface; usually contains yarns of

more than one color, or of different shades of the
same color.

Unfinished Worsted. Worsted wool fabric with slight
nap surface which obscures the weave.

Velour. Soft, closely woven fabric with short thick
pile similar to velvet, made from wool fibers.

Vicuña. Fibers of the fur of the vicuña, a South American animal related to the llama, extremely light
in weight and usually combined with other wool
fibers to weave luxurious fabrics.

Virgin Wool. Wool which has never been used for yarn
or fabric before, or for any other purpose.

Viyella. A wool and cotton fabric, very light in weight;
the two yarns are blended before spinning.

Whipcord. Twill-weave fabric similar to gabardine
with a more pronounced rib; of wool fibers.

Wool. The hair of sheep, lambs, and other similar ani-
mals which is spun, woven, or knitted into fabrics.

Woolen. Fabric woven or knitted from carded wool,
more loosely twisted than *worsted wool,* conse-
quently having a more fuzzy surface.

Worsted. Fabric woven from evenly combed, long
staple yarns, tightly twisted and woven and having a smoother surface than other woolen fabrics.

Sewing with Synthetics

Because there are so many new man-made fibers
today, with more appearing every season, it is advisable to inquire when purchasing fabrics what they are
comprised of and how to "handle" them. That is, how
to launder or dry clean them, what kind of thread to
use, how sun-fast or color-fast they are, and how much

they stretch or shrink. Most synthetic materials are
said to be "stable"—neither stretching nor shrinking;
but since there are also many "knit" weaves, which do
stretch, and "crepe" weaves, which can present stitching problems, learn as much as you can about them
before buying.

Among the most common fibers available now are
the machine-washable, machine-dryable *polyesters.*
Some are medium-weight crepes, with good drape
qualities; these are suitable for fairly dressy garments
such as dresses, blouses, full-length jumpsuits, full
slacks, and at-home clothes.

Another polyester machine-washable, machine-
dryable fabric comes in a *knit* texture similar
to jersey. It comes in a number of weights, some almost as thin as a nylon stocking, others heavy enough
for tailored suits and even coats.

Most of the polyesters have good features not always found in other fabrics. They hang well, do not
wrinkle readily, they are easy to sew, and of course,
they wash beautifully. Like most knits, polyesters snag
rather easily. Very lightweight polyesters are just as
difficult to handle as any other lightweight fabric.

Because of the nature of synthetic fibers, the colors
in man-made fabrics are not as good as those of natural-fiber cloth. Apart from this, they are good materials to start sewing with, particularly in the
recommended medium weights. Because synthetics
wash well and require no ironing, even the most complicated garment will keep its shape indefinitely.

Some synthetics retain grease spots. If normal
washing does not remove a spot, mark it with thread
before wetting and apply mild soap to the area, taking care not to remove or rough up the surface of the

cloth with too much friction. Most bleaches are dangerous for synthetics but Snowy normally works. White synthetics tend to turn gray or grimy with repeated washing, so a good program of mild bleaching with every laundering will help prevent this. Watch all light-colored synthetics for signs of griminess and take steps to correct them. One way is to wash them separately and *never* mix badly soiled garments with lightly soiled things. Man-made fibers seem to attract any loose dirt or color dissolved in the wash water.

Before washing or bleaching any garment you have made, be it synthetic or natural fiber, it is wise to experiment with a scrap to determine the best way to handle it. Temperature in the washing machine, as well as in the dryer, should be moderate for synthetic fabrics.

Keep a record of all the information you can get on each fabric; one way to do this is to staple or tape a two-inch by four-inch scrap of the cloth to a file card on which you have written the date of purchase, the fiber content and all other pertinent information. Keep these cards near the washing machine and compare the garment with the scrap from time to time to check changes in color. This will help you to learn the good qualities of various fabrics. Take into consideration the number of launderings each garment has had when making comparisons.

Sewing a synthetic-fiber fabric is not very different from sewing a natural-fiber fabric. Always use a *sharp needle* of the correct size in the sewing machine. The right weight of *thread* is important, too. Threads developed especially for knits are good if you remember that they can *melt* under a hot iron. Take care when pressing seams to use the proper setting on the iron, and use a pressing cloth if you are in doubt. Once more, experiment with a scrap to determine the exact temperature for your fabric and thread.

There are other synthetics besides polyester, under many names. *Nylon, rayon* and *celanese* are fairly common and each has some good characteristics, some bad. Nylon is generally very thin and therefore difficult for the seamstress to handle. If you are prepared to be patient it may be worthwhile. Some of the nylon prints are sensational in color and design. The pattern you use must be suitable for this clinging, often "sleazy" fabric. In plain colors, nylon jersey may look a little too much like lingerie.

Rayon represents a group of synthetic fabrics which have been improved since they were first created, and are now comparable in many ways to the traditional fabrics that they attempted to supplement. For example, inexpensive silks were used for linings until synthetics were invented. However, as silk became more costly, synthetics replaced it. Synthetics have been improved so much that there are man-made, inexpensive materials for nearly every purpose.

Although synthetics are generally less expensive than the natural fabrics they are replacing, there are disadvantages to many of them which should be understood. Nearly every kind of natural fiber has been copied, and the "look" and "feel" that are an important part of the beauty of the fabrics are simulated in the copies. However, they are still copies. Real linen still looks different from linen-textured rayon. Most rayon ravels excessively. In an effort to reduce wrinkling, the manufacturers have made some of the rayon fabrics wiry. There is a shiny look to rayon which identifies it and tends to look rather cheap.

On the good side, there are many fabrics which have their own individual attractions not copied from something else. Study both the "feel" and the "hang" of these materials and take note of the raveling on the cut edge. If you sew with these fabrics, take care to finish all edges as soon as they are cut to reduce this tendency. A fabric which ravels readily may pull apart under strain, so avoid making very tight-fitting garments when using these materials.

Names of Synthetics

The names of synthetic fabrics and terms related to them are listed here:

Acetate. Applied to fabric, fibers, yarns and threads made of cellulose acetate.

Acrylic Fibers. Synthetic fibers made from thermoplastic resins.

Alginate Rayon. Fibers produced from alginic acid, derived from seaweed.

Azlon. Fibers made from proteins such as milk, corn and soybeans.

Casein Fibers. Fibers produced from skimmed milk and made to resemble wool.

Cellulose. Vegetable fiber used in the manufacture of rayon and acetate.

Continuous Filament. Synthetic fibers can be manufactured in a continuous filament—that is, a long thread—in contrast to the short fibers of natural materials such as linen and wool.

Denier. Term indicating size or number of a filament or yarn, as applied to man-made fibers or silk, that is determined by the number of .05 gram weights (deniers) of a standard skein of 450 meters. The higher the denier number the coarser the yarn.

Hand. The "feel" of a fabric, referring to its flexibility, resilience, and draping quality.

Nylon. Polyamide fiber.

Pellon. Non-woven interlining material made in several weights.

Rayon. Fibers made from regenerated cellulose.

Synthetic Fibers. Textile fibers made by chemical synthesis; man-made fibers; fibers with cellulose base are rayon and acetate. Fibers with protein base are Vicaras. Fibers with chemical base are nylon, Dacron, Acrilan, and Dynel.

6

Lace and Trimmings

The fringed trim on the poncho Irv is
wearing adds a professional touch.
The poncho is made of red, beige, gray,
and white wool.

6
Lace and Trimmings

One of the principal fabrics not described in the foregoing chapters is lace. Lace can be made with several kinds of fibers. Originally it was made of cotton, silk, or linen, but today many laces are made in synthetic yarns on the same machines that formerly made laces from natural fibers.

The problems you will encounter when sewing with lace are far from serious, and you should certainly consider lace and its near relatives, embroidered fabrics, when selecting fabrics to sew.

For a complete garment, such as a blouse, there are many kinds of *over-all laces* wide enough to use with any pattern. These include cotton lace in floral designs and some geometric designs which are adaptable to less dressy garments.

Embroidered materials such as eyelet, which is fresh and youthful, and embroidered linen, which is elegant and dressy, can be used for a wide range of garments. The more luxurious laces made in silk or nylon are suited more to formal gowns and wedding dresses. The beginning sewer may not feel quite up to this kind of task, although I don't see why you couldn't make your own wedding dress if you are willing to forego the more difficult kinds of fabric. Many wedding dresses have been made of delicate cotton, eyelet, or lace.

Sewing with Lace

Apart from the many over-all lace materials which are not difficult to sew, there are many narrow laces and embroideries which should be considered. A band of wide lace around the skirt of a simple dress can transform it into something special. A lace collar and cuffs can do miracles with a plain black dress. The front of a simple blouse can be pepped up with vertical rows of crisp embroidered edging, ruffled, flat, or tailored. You will think of hundreds of ways to enrich a simple dress with lace.

Sewing with lace presents some individual problems based on the weight and transparency of the material. In general, the coarser cotton laces can be treated in the same manner as other lightweight cotton fabrics. If the inside of the seam, the seam-allowance, is visible through the openings in the lace, it will not matter in most places, such as side seams and skirt seams. You may want to *bind seams* which are close to the top of the garment, however, such as the seams of the armholes. You may even want to bind the underarm seam down to the waistline, if the dress is two-piece. Do whatever looks good: if you don't like the looks of the seam-allowance, trim it off and bind the seam with a fine grade of cotton bias tape. Or, you can use bias strips you make yourself out of the thinnest cotton you can comfortably handle.

For silk and nylon lace, make sure the material is stiff enough to handle. The slippery and soft "feel" of thin materials will guide you in this matter, for you will always have difficulty putting two cut pieces together when the fabric is extremely thin and does not hold its shape.

If the pattern you are using has buttons, *don't* attempt to make buttonholes in lace. Either sew buttons on top with snaps underneath or use loops on the edge of the placket. If the lace is very open and a button happens to fall right over a hole, use a thin cotton interlining between the right side of the garment and the part of the opening that is turned under.

Usually lace is not good for facing itself at armholes and necklines. When you buy the lace, select a fine cotton fabric in the closest possible match in color (yes, you have to match white, too) to use even if the garment has its own collar. The neck facing will still have to be made of plain goods. Another good reason for facing the lace with cotton is that it will be more comfortable next to the skin, especially if the lace is coarse.

The material you use for facing will be suitable for cutting into bias strips if you have to bind a seam. Even if a lace garment has sleeves, always bind the armhole.

Make the hem in a lace dress much wider than the hem in a dress of opaque material.

If the lace you are trying to sew catches in the presser foot of the machine, lay a strip of tissue paper on top as you sew. You may have to baste this paper on, if the seam is complicated, or you may find that you can tape it in place. *Always* experiment on a scrap to see if the tape will come off without damaging the fabric. If you are sewing a seam which will later be bound, such as the armhole seam, baste the sleeve in carefully and then baste on the binding. Stitch once, through the binding, using a small stitch. And use care.

Sewing with Trimmings

In addition to the great variety of laces, both the over-all laces and the various widths of border types, there is another entire class of textiles that should be considered when shopping for a do-it-yourself wardrobe. These are the almost infinite variety of *trims* under the heading of *edgings, embroidered* and *beaded braids,* woven *galloons* and printed *borders.*

Almost any character of trim, from the most opulent gold embroideries embellished with beads, tiny mirrors, cordonnets, and sequins to the peasant embroideries of hearts and bright red and blue flowers of Swiss mountaineers, can give you great help in creating costumes. The simplest straight dress of a fine shantung, for example, with a yoke outlined in Indian embroidery, becomes an elegant costume, perfect for a wedding reception or the most exclusive dining place in town. When you are looking at patterns, consider the endless variations you can make in the basic design with the clever use of trim.

Trims vary in the way they are handled. The more expensive embroideries, often made in India and the Orient, are heavier, and require a fabric of body to support and complement them. They should be sewed onto the finished or partly finished dress *by hand,* using the blind hemming stitch you use for sleeve and skirt hems. If you use such a border embroidery to outline a square yoke, for example, the shoulder seam should be left open or ripped to allow the braid to be caught in to the seam, rather than require turning under on itself to finish it, unless the braid continues around the neck across the back.

If the braid is used around the hem or around a sleeve, it should be placed *above* the actual edge of the garment rather than on the exact edge, except in such traditional cases as kaftans, where the trim is always found on the edge. The edge of such a garment is usually either a printed border design or an intrinsic part of the woven pattern of the garment.

When using narrow Bavarian, Austrian, or Swiss type braid, use more than one row or combine the braid with straight *soutache braid* (Hungarian design) or *rickrack* in solid colors matching the embroidered braid. Adding this trim will keep the trim from looking skimpy or out of scale, unless the braid itself "carries" well and is really important. This applies to any trim or lace—if it looks skimpy it will defeat the purpose. The exception is baby clothes, of course, where delicacy is a desirable quality.

Many flat cotton braids can be sewed on by machine, even with the zigzag if you like the extra touch. Warning: all braids on washable garments should be *preshrunk*. Always buy a half yard more than you need and wash the trim in hot water, both to find out if it runs and to shrink it. Don't stretch the braid to press it. This applies to rickrack, too. Failing to wash and press the braid will result in the puckering of all trims because the chances are remote that they will shrink the same as the fabric to which they are sewed. And take care not to stretch rickrack or any bias braid when sewing it on.

Use a fairly long stitch with thread to match the braid or a contrasting color if you want to emphasize the line. If there is not too much braid, it's a good idea to sew it on by hand, even for cotton braid, because you can stretch it slightly as you sew, especially on curves. If you have plenty of time, braid looks terrific sewed on with such embroidery stitches as blanket stitch and feather stitch.

Because most trims are woven straight, they don't go around curves easily. Try to design the application of straight trims along straight lines; where curves are unavoidable, use the largest possible radius. Make *mitered corners* and sharp turns. Practice making miters which don't cut into the principal parts of the design; have the same motif on each side of the diagonal corner.

The effect of trims is enhanced if they are not used in cut-up chunks. Instead of placing just a strip across the top of a pocket, outline the whole pocket with the braid. This will give greater impact to the pockets as decorative features and to the trim itself. Balance the placement on the garment to "echo" itself; in other words, if there is a concentration of trim around the neck, use a smaller "echoing" amount on sleeves or pockets, or vice versa. Avoid exactly similar amounts in two places—that is boring. Sometimes, if the braid is very important, as in the case of wide Indian trims, one location is enough.

If you want to go still further in enriching a simple garment, try picking out the design on an embroidered trim with tiny beads or pearls. Do this after the whole garment is finished and start in the front, so that if you get tired of it, you can stop. Just a few points of sparkle on an important dress give punch. Don't plan on reworking the whole design—pick one spot, the center of a flower, for example, and put two or three

Figure 4. Ideas for Trimming Children's Clothes

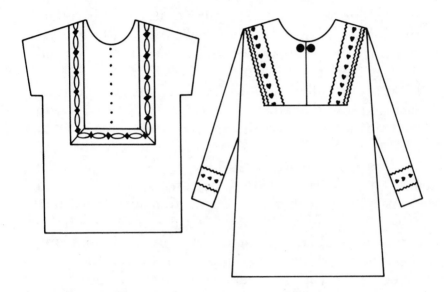

Mitered Corners

Trimming with Ribbon

faceted beads in each one. The whole trim will come to life. Judicious use of sequins can do this too, but avoid a concentration of sequins unless you are going all out for drama and a theatrical effect. If this is what will work, you can buy sequin borders by the yard all the way from two rows to a yard wide.

Many so-called "ethnic" types of garments can be enriched and embellished with borders. Not only do the traditional fabrics themselves often come printed with borders but there are some woven or printed borders which work with these textiles. Most of the African prints are made in cotton, and cotton braid looks best with them. If you make a woolen kaftan, however, consider trimming it with a woven wool border in a geometric design. Sometimes, if you look ahead when cutting out this kind of fabric, such as a striped wool, you can reserve a section, like one prominent stripe in a strong color, for a border. Or use crosswise stripes to form a border on a lengthwise striped garment.

One place you may forget to look, when shopping for borders and trims, is the drapery department in big stores. However, the whole spectrum of house-furnishing fabrics comes in quite a different range of colors from dress goods. Take samples of a trim you like down to the dress-fabric department for comparison before trying to match colors. Even whites are different and it may turn out you have to change the basic material of your garment, if you really find a trim you must have.

Still another department is the ribbon counter. For garments which will be dry-cleaned, French damask ribbon is spectacular for its soft colors and rich designs, and there are numerous ribbed and striped ribbons in wonderful colors. They can be used for contrasting scarves, for example, in wide widths, and sashes or belts. If you make a belt from ribbon, sew the ribbon to a backing of belting material, because it will curl or wrinkle by itself.

If you decide to use a certain trim with a certain fabric, plan ahead a little. Take out the pattern and make up your mind where the braid is going. This way you can measure the amount needed.

When you decide where the trim is going, mark your pattern before placing it on the fabric. Use a strip of paper, about as heavy as letter paper, as wide as the trim. Lay it on top of the pattern where you are going to sew the braid and lightly trace along the edges of the paper. Let the trim run to the edge of the pattern, into the seam-allowance, if the construction of the garment calls for the trim to cross seams.

When placing a strip or strips of trim around the bottom of a skirt, measure up from the bottom frequently to make sure you are exactly parallel to the bottom; this is not a straight line but a long arc. Don't forget to measure up from the intended *finished hem line*, not the actual bottom of the pattern. Place the trim above the fold of the hem.

When basting on the trim, later, it may be necessary to stretch it slightly when going around curves. On washable, preshrunk braid, a little steaming will remove some of the wrinkles, but they can safely be ignored in most cases, especially if the trim is rather heavy.

When you mark the trim lines on the fabric, don't forget that the lines to follow for trimming have to be on the *right* side of the fabric. If possible, use carbon paper and cover the marks as you sew on the braid so they won't show.

Except where the trim will end inside a seam, you can sew it on after the dress is finished if you like. It will look more tailored if it has been finished and steamed before any other stitching, however. These decisions are really based on the type of trim and the kind of material used; on washable fabric with cotton braid, everything can be done before you sew the dress together. When using very expensive or metallic braid, especially wide braid, it is better to wait until the end. Besides, less of this kind of braid is used and it is always sewed by hand in any case.

No special care need be given to preshrunk cotton braid other than gentle pressing after laundering. With expensive braid *always* call attention to the braid when taking it to the dry cleaner and instruct him to use extreme care in both cleaning and pressing it. Don't press this kind of braid yourself without experimenting first on a scrap; you will almost always have to use a press-cloth. Sometimes you can press on the wrong side, through the garment, with a Turkish towel laid over the ironing board, to prevent pressing down the design too much. Avoid imprinting the braid on other parts of the garment.

Other forms of trimming include fringe, appliqué and embroidery. Contrasting colors of different kinds, including prints on plain and plain on prints, present almost unlimited possibilities. As you collect a scrap bag you will see opportunities to use this kind of trim, particularly if you have really coordinated your wardrobe, and the fabrics are related. You may find that a belt of another material, a scarf, or a tie is all you want to pep up a simple dress. Keep a scrapbook of things you see in magazines to help create a good supply of ideas and to stimulate your own imagination when planning a garment.

Names of Laces

Lace is a fine netting or openwork fabric of linen, cotton, or silk threads—forming an ornamental design, either overall or border pattern; originally made entirely by hand, it is now made by hand, by machine, or both; often refers to narrow (one-half inch to three inches) trimming material of lace construction, used either straight or gathered. Types of lace are as follows:

Alençon. Delicate but durable lace with solid designs outlined with cord on a sheer net background; machine-made Alençon in good grades has this cord applied by hand.

All-over Lace. Wide lace fabric up to thirty-six inches wide, with pattern repeated over the whole surface; sometimes has border design on one or both edges.

Aloe Lace. Fragile lace made of aloe plant fibers in Philippines and Italy.

Antique Lace. Handmade lace, made with bobbins and heavy thread, in large knotted net with darned designs.

Battenberg. A form of Renaissance lace, made of linen braid or tape formed into designs by stitching between the loops of tape.

Binche Lace. Flemish bobbin lace of stars, snowflake patterns, and scroll floral designs, rather fine.

Breton Lace. Net with heavy designs embroidered on it, sometimes in colors.

Chantilly Lace. Bobbin lace, originally of silk, now often nylon, with fine mesh background and delicate designs outlined with cordonnet of thicker silk threads.

Cluny Lace. Rather heavy bobbin lace with wheel motif, or a poinsettia; of heavy threads.

Dresden Point Lace. Drawnwork in linen, with some threads interlaced and embroidered, forming square meshes.

Irish Lace. Crocheted lace and net embroideries, especially those of Limerick and Carrickmacross.

Lille Lace. Fine bobbin lace, often dotted, with designs outlined in flat cordonnet.

Malines. Very fine silk net, extremely diaphanous.

Milan Lace. Tape lace with needle-point mesh and picot edging.

Needle-point Lace. Handmade lace, worked over a paper pattern entirely with a sewing needle, using buttonhole and blanket stitches.

Renaissance Lace. Lace formed by using a variety of flat stitches to join continuous-tape designs.

Rose Point Lace. Venetian needle-point lace of delicate texture, in floral, foliage, and scroll designs connected with string cordonnet.

Spanish Lace. Heavy flat floral designs held together by various meshes, made only in Spain, usually of silk.

Tatting. Handmade lace, made by using a shuttle and the fingers, mostly in geometric designs.

Val or Valenciennes Lace. Flat bobbin lace, the background and the design formed with the same thread, originally from linen; now made in cotton, with either round or diamond mesh; common lace edgings used for lingerie and children's clothes usually called "val" lace.

Venice Lace. A needle-point lace with floral patterns connected with irregular picot edges.

7
Color

Modern clothes designs often use
unusual color and print combinations.
Here Luis wears an African-printed
cotton shirt of red, black, and yellow
cotton. The trousers are yellow and
black.

7
Color

Whatever the fiber content or structure of a fabric, the most important feature is surely *color*. Even the most stylish garment created with expert workmanship can fail if the color is unbecoming. Color can complement skin tones and hair color, or turn them muddy and lifeless. Knowing how to look at color in relation to your own coloring is the most important part of selecting dress fabrics.

When you buy a ready-made dress, you try it on and study yourself in a mirror; do the same with a fabric. Hold the material in front of you, covering all the garments you have on. Try to look at the fabric in the kind of light you will wear it under, that is, daylight for street clothes and artificial light for evening things.

You may think you know what colors are becoming to you. Good. But there are many shades of every color. Don't make the mistake of lumping all blues together, for example, and taking it for granted that you look good in blue. Blue can run from green-blue to purple-blue, from navy to baby. Some blues are "raw" and extremely hard to wear, indeed all "raw" colors are hard to wear. This rawness is often the result of a high concentration of pigment and referred to as "bright," but this is not necessarily correct, for white can be "bright" with no color at all. Brightness should not be confused with this quality of harshness which is generally found in cheap goods. Synthetic fibers are more difficult to dye than natural fibers, and many cheap synthetics have this "raw" look, but cheap natural fibers don't look much better, for other reasons. Remember that you are not only spending money when you shop for dress material, but you are going to spend time and effort; invest wisely. *Buy the best you can afford in any category.*

Analyze Yourself

Above all, when selecting colors, know your own skin and hair tones. Most women have had at least one session with a trained cosmetician who has analyzed her coloring and recommended proper makeup. Once you know your basic skin color, make a fair-sized sample of the *base color* to compare with fabrics. You can vary lipstick and eye coloring with the color you are wearing; indeed, this is imperative if you want to blend the entire color scheme professionally. If you don't wear makeup, you still have to consider skin color, eye color and hair color. It is difficult to overemphasize the importance of color interaction. Painters spend years studying what colors do to each other and developing techniques of juxtaposition. The first step to successful color selection for a garment, whether you buy it or make it, is to know what happens to your own coloring when you put other colors next to it.

If your skin changes in the summer from suntan you must take this into consideration when planning summer clothes. If you change your hair color you should take another look at yourself in relation to colors—the old favorites might not make it any longer.

The thing to do is always look for *color harmony*. Although *color harmony* is a complex and serious study, there are some basic guidelines which will help you to know what you are doing when you look for colors which combine well with your skin, hair and eye tones.

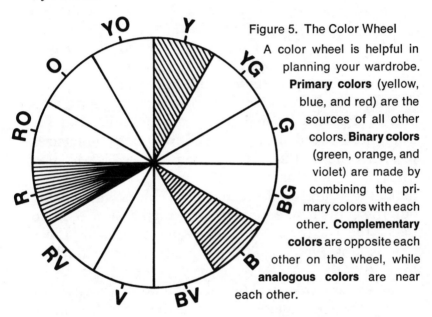

Figure 5. The Color Wheel

A color wheel is helpful in planning your wardrobe. **Primary colors** (yellow, blue, and red) are the sources of all other colors. **Binary colors** (green, orange, and violet) are made by combining the primary colors with each other. **Complementary colors** are opposite each other on the wheel, while **analogous colors** are near each other.

Colors are either *analogous* or *complementary*. For example, blue and green are analogous because they are similar; green is a combination of blue and another color. Colors which are similar or close together produce restful, soothing color schemes. Blue and orange are complementary; neither color has any of the other in its composition. Colors which are opposite or far apart produce stimulating color schemes.

Complementary colors tend to emphasize each other; if they are bright to start with, they may be even brighter side-by-side. But changes occur when any two colors are combined, whether or not they are complementary. Muddy colors tend to fade out the value or depth of adjoining colors, particularly if the adjoining color is lighter, less saturated. Strong colors can overpower weaker or lighter colors, draining them of distinction.

Since in the case of light skin tones, strong colors can produce a sallow effect, care should be used in the selection of assertive shades. Dark-skinned women do not have a much easier problem. Some very bright colors bring out too much red, for example, in brown skin tones, giving an undesirable ruddy effect.

Most shades of brown skin look very good in all shades of cream, beige, ivory, and non-reddish tan, for example. Any red, orange, or yellow which emphasizes reddish tones in the skin, whether or not it is so-called brown or only a dark shade of "white," is inclined to make the wearer look warm; those colors which bring out the bluish or greenish tints in the skin tend to make the wearer look cool. Watch the latter for a muddy look, which isn't desirable for anyone, dark or fair.

When considering fabrics composed of two or more colors, the same general effects can be anticipated. The overall color effect of a print, the color you see if you squint a little, is the one to study. Or in large, bold prints, study the dominating color.

What Colors Do for You

Casual clothes and sports clothes can usually be made in brighter colors than those suitable for business or street wear, though there are no hard and fast rules.

Red is certainly a bright color in many cases, but

is regarded as a "standard" all-year-round basic color, like *black* and *navy*. Since there are hundreds, even thousands, of shades of red, you should be able to find a number of becoming shades, suitable for your coloring.

The easiest colors for light-skinned girls to wear are the *orange-reds*, which are analogous to the warm tones in their skin. This includes *lacquer, vermillion,* and *flame-reds*. Dark-skinned women look good in these and the *blue-reds*, like *carmine, cerise,* and *shocking*. Everyone should take care to avoid the harsh *purplish-reds* which are unbecoming to most skin-tones, be they light or dark.

Red combines well with many other colors, especially *white, blue,* and *yellow*. In tropical color schemes, involving vivid primary colors, red is sometimes used in bold combinations with *green, orange,* and *purple;* unless you are an expert in color harmony, beware of the indiscriminate use of such strong combinations. They can call attention to themselves at the expense of the wearer.

Although *green* has a reputation for being hard to wear, this is true only of certain greens with certain skin tones. Dark-skinned women, for example, can wear almost all shades of green, because brown and green are a variation of both the complementary color scheme and the analogous color scheme. Brown is essentially a warm color, composed of red modified by *blue* and *yellow;* green contains no red at all. The nearer to yellow the green is, the closer it is to an alliance with the *yellow* tones in the brown skin; the closer to blue-green, the more it works with the *blue* tones in the brown.

Light-colored skin, on the other hand, contains less

concentrated colors, and green can emphasize some undesirable undertones, such as a yellowish look, or a bluish look, especially if the green is a saturated color itself. In general, soft *blue-greens* are easiest to wear, but this is subject to experiment with specific skin colorings.

Women with red hair often have vivid coloring and some shades of green are sensational on them, because the same thing happens for them that happens for brown-skinned girls. However, since this results in a strong complementary color scheme, discretion is urged.

Blue is an adaptable color; some shade of blue will look good on everyone. About the only blue to be afraid of is a highly saturated royal, or other "raw" harsh blue. Brown-skinned girls look good in shades of blue from *turquoise*, a greenish blue, to *periwinkle*, a pinkish blue. Blue is like green. On dark skin, it can be the most becoming color possible.

Fair-skinned girls need only avoid shades of blue which tend to make them look pale or colorless; this can be compensated for by using a slightly warmer shade of makeup, in some cases. Blue eyeshadow is great with a blue dress. Needless to say, girls with blue eyes find blue especially becoming, since most shades of blue will emphasize eye color.

Yellow is hard on a sallow skin but looks great on clear skin tones, both fair and dark. Like its near neighbor, *cream*, it is good on brown skin if the shade of yellow is not too garish. Soft shades of nearly all colors look best on dark skin tones; this is because two dark colors together reinforce each other, while a dark and light color together can harmonize, to the advantage of both.

Yellow looks good on blondes, if the shade of yellow is harmonious with the hair color and does not make the skin tones look colorless. All light skin tones have yellow in them; the trick is to bring out the warmth without making the skin turn sallow or muddy against the color of the dress.

Orange has some of the qualities of both red and yellow, being composed of the two colors in various mixtures. Whatever happens to the skin tones with red will happen with *red-orange*, only more so. The yellow skin tones will echo the yellow in the orange. A high-contrast effect results from orange against dark skin; this is another case of two strong colors reinforcing each other. The softer shades of orange look very good with dark skin, and with lighter skin tones as well. The right shade of orange is very good with pale blonde hair, especially if the skin is very clear.

The right shade of orange, very close to the hair color, can be striking on a redhead. The exact shade of the hair color, be it red or brown or gray, makes a striking costume, heightening the skin color in most cases, if the hair color itself is right for the skin tones.

Purple is sometimes overlooked as a possible choice for ordinary clothing because of its traditional association with royalty and the church. Nevertheless, there are many shades of purple: *violet, lavender*, and all sorts of *blue-violet* shades, as well as the pale pinkish-lavender tones, which are hard to pass up. Purple is notoriously hard to wear, and care should be used in selecting any of these colors in solid tones. Checks, stripes, and of course prints, are easier to use. Women with red hair should certainly watch out for the garish effect of purple and red! Although women with gray hair look very good in pale shades of most colors, this should not discourage young women, especially pale blondes, from trying subtle shades of violet and lavender for unusual color schemes. The effect of lavender or any purple on the skin is to emphasize the blue or lavender which underlies light-colored skin. Dark skin often has bluish undertones too, so the dark-skinned girl has to study the total effect, too.

Gray is a color in a class of its own, for its color is less important than its shade. It ranges from *charcoal gray*, which is nearly black, to *pearl gray*, which is nearly white. Since it contains a diluted and modified mixture of other colors, it can be judged pretty much by the same standards.

If you like blue, you might like *bluish-gray*. Gray is a basic, year-round color like black, navy, and red. It can be worn by nearly everyone in some shade or other. It combines well with other colors, making it suitable for coats, suits, skirts, and slacks. When looking for colors to wear with gray, you will find that all the colors contained in the gray itself, for example, the blues in bluish-gray, will blend well with it. Crossing over to the other side, trying to match reds and oranges with bluish-gray can also work well, producing a somewhat brighter contrasting effect. About the most important thing in selecting gray is getting the most becoming shade. If you wear makeup, you can usually wear a little brighter eye-shadow and a little warmer tone of base and powder with gray.

Basic-color Wardrobe

For a beginning seamstress, a pair of gray wool knit slacks or a gray flannel skirt would make a good first project for fall or winter. For spring, a gray linen jumper to wear with print blouses could be worn in hot weather alone with only a scarf. Gray fits in most wardrobes without friction.

Black is basic. Few women would consider their wardrobe complete without at least one "good" black dress. Most people can wear black; most women feel "dressed up" in black. Black brings out the undertones of warmth in dark skin. It contrasts dramatically with light skin. The right makeup can correct the effect of black on sallow skin, helping to alleviate the somewhat hardening effect of unrelieved black. Actually, black looks best as a background for jewels or accessories, especially if they are striking in themselves and the dress is simple. Black also makes a dramatic foil for white.

Contrary to what you might expect, there are many shades of black. The blackest black is usually found in the most expensive fabrics, principally yarn-dyed wool or silk. Black cotton will not keep its blackness with repeated washing, and turns out rather grayish after a while.

There are few occasions where black is not appropriate. However, for active sports and for very warm days in summer, it is not a logical choice, since it absorbs heat more than any other color. Considering the prevalence of air-conditioning, black is acceptable for indoor and evening wear, and because it always looks smart, many women will suffer a little for its sake.

Brown is considered a "basic" color like black or navy blue, but it is harder to wear. It comes in many shades and tones and presents problems like any color. What does it do to the skin tones? It does the same thing as any other color, only it is not quite as pronounced, since it contains all the other colors mixed together in various proportions. Women with very dark skin look good in brown because it is analogous with the tones of the skin. However, brown with much red in it can make dark skin unpleasantly ruddy.

Women with light skin have to watch the ruddy effect, too, together with a muddy look which is even worse. If the hair color and general skin color contain the same kind of brown undertones, then brown will look good. However, most very warm brown tones can have a disasterous effect on sallow skin, making it lifeless.

Accessories in brown can be found during most seasons and combine well with other colors, so brown finds its way into the wardrobe, even if brown dresses and blouses are not too becoming. Creamy beiges and tans, yellow and orange, and a number of greens harmonize with brown, so it can be successfully introduced into the color scheme if you like it.

Names of Dyes and Printing

Fabrics are given their colors and patterns by certain dyes and ways of printing. The following list names some of them:

Alizarin Dye. Vegetable dye derived from the madder root, very resistant to fading from sun and washing; usually used on wool; now synthesized.

Aniline Dyes. Any dye derived chemically from aniline or other coal tar products.

Batik. A method of resist dyeing originating in Java.

The design is created by coating parts of the cloth with wax, which will remain clear while the rest of the fabric absorbs the dye. The process can be repeated to dye more than one color over the former color. Batik is characterized by the streaks which result from cracks in the wax which allow some of the dye to penetrate the masked areas. Batik is sometimes imitated in machine printing.

Bleaching. Process to remove impurities in fabrics before dyeing or printing; can be done with sunlight or chemicals; increases the fabric's ability to absorb and retain dyes.

Bleeding. The dye in some textiles will run or "bleed" during washing, especially if there is an excess of dye. (See Madras, Chapter 4.)

Cochineal. Brilliant red dye obtained from dried cochineal insects.

Crocking. Term for what happens when the excess dye in some fabrics, particularly napped and pile textiles in dark colors, rubs off.

Dyeing. The process of coloring either fibers or fabrics with natural or chemical (synthetic) dyes. Dyes vary widely in their resistance to fading under exposure to sunlight, gases, washing methods, or other causes, and in their reaction to water, perspiration, cleaning agents, and other liquids, as well as in their ability to permeate fibers or textiles evenly.

Indigo. The oldest known vat dye, obtained from the indigo plant; now synthesized; shades produced by indigo cannot be duplicated with any other substances; very resistant to light and washing.

Tie Dyeing. The fabric is tied with string, often over

some shaped cardboard or wood, then dyed—the tied parts do not absorb the dye and produce the design; random dyeing; done by hand.

Vat Dye. Insoluble dye, reduced during the application to the fiber to a soluble form, then oxidized to restore the dye to its insoluble form; most resistant to light and washing of all dyes.

Yarn Dyeing. Dyed in the fiber before weaving or knitting the fabric.

Duplex Print. Method of printing both sides of the fabric so that the design is the same on both sides.

Hand-Blocked Print. Printing on fabrics by hand with wood or linoleum blocks.

India Print. Muslin (cotton fabric) printed with designs from traditional Indian motifs in glowing oriental colors, done with wood blocks by hand.

Jouy or *Toile de Jouy.* Cotton fabric printed with one-color reproductions of 18-century etchings showing landscapes and figures.

Piece Dyeing. Dyeing woven fabrics.

Photographic Printing. Application of photo image on cloth.

Printing. Designs on fabric; called *block printing* if done with blocks, *hand block printing* if the blocks are carved by hand and the process of printing is done by hand, as in India prints; most commercial fabrics are *roller-printed;* some fine silks and cottons are *screen-printed,* sometimes by hand on silk screens.

Resist Printing. The principle used in batik dyeing; substances which do not absorb dye are applied in designs, the fabric is dipped in dye and the "resist" substance is removed.

Screen Printing. Printing similar to stenciling; the

background of the design is blocked out with paste and the dye is printed through the exposed parts of the screen; each color is on a separate screen with different blocking out.

Shadow Print. The warp yarns only are printed in the design, giving a watery or faint effect; warp print.

8

Putting It All Together

Meredith wears a red dress of polyester
knit. The dress has a yoke cut on the
bias, a back zipper, and patch pockets.

8

Putting It All Together

If you already know how to operate a sewing machine, this chapter will not interest you. If you have not had much practice, however, start your first garment by learning how to stitch *accurately, straight,* and *evenly* before tackling the actual garment itself.

If you have nothing else to practice on, use the scraps you would normally throw away after cutting out the dress. Pin them together, two at a time, edges together. The pins should be at right angles to the cut edge of the cloth with the point not closer than a half inch from the edge. Most machines stitch over pins, but if the pins are not exactly at right angles to the line of stitching, sometimes the needle breaks.

Never stitch on a single layer of cloth unless you are zigzagging the edge. (See Chapter 9.)

If your machine does not have a line on the bed of the machine, at the right of the needle, to indicate various *seam-allowance* widths, make a line yourself. Measure five-eighths of an inch to the right of the point directly under the needle and lay a strip of adhesive tape or masking tape on this line, parallel to the left edge of the machine, from front to back. This line will help you to maintain an even margin on seams with the usual five-eighths inch allowance. However, lines are no substitute for the indispensable ability to stitch accurately, which can come only from practice. So practice. It may take hours, even days, but since a fairly bright eight-year-old can master this skill, you can.

Stitching

Settle down with your scraps and keep practicing until you can operate the machine on straight lines and on curves. Draw lines with a ruler at first, and practice keeping on the line; for curves, trace the edge of a dinner plate. Baste some of the scraps together and follow the basting line.

Sometimes the edge snarls when you place the fabric under the needle to begin stitching because the needle does not have enough material to get a good grip for the first stitch. To avoid this, push the fabric a little beyond the point where the needle will go. And *do not forget to lower the presser foot*.

The left hand should help to hold the material in place, but should not *pull* the fabric through the machine. The right hand should guide the fabric, keeping the stitching line straight. In the case of very thin fabrics and knits, it is necessary to hold the material more firmly, even to stretch it slightly.

Experiment with each fabric. Make sure the *tension* on the machine is adjusted to fit the weight of the material and that the best *stitch length* has been determined. The smaller the stitch, the greater the chance for puckering the fabric. The longest stitch, however, is suitable only for basting, and not recommended for final stitching.

Make sure you are using the *right size of needle*,

too. After a little practice, you will be able to anticipate the various adjustments needed for any kind of material. There is no good substitute for experience.

When you can handle the mechanics of operating the sewing machine, you can start to sew. *Don't* practice learning how to stitch on the first garment; use the scraps. Nothing is more disheartening than ripping. Ripping is time-consuming, frustrating, irritating, ego-deflating, tension-producing, and difficult. It's not too good for the garment, either. It may even be impossible to remove the stitching marks.

The best way to steer clear of ripping is to *baste.* Basting is not wasting time. Think of basting as foundation work, like the caissons under a high-rise building. Without a good start, few things come to a good end. So baste.

No matter how well you work, you will have to rip once in a while. Rip carefully when you do, because it is easy to spoil the fabric with hasty ripping. If you use the ripper gadget, and it has much to recommend it, avoid cutting the material. Press or steam out the stitch marks as soon as possible. Rip out machine stitching before stitching again; it is very difficult to rip threads which have been stitched over.

Working with the Pattern

Simple-to-Make patterns are easy to put together. The instruction sheets which come with the patterns are clear, detailed, well-illustrated, and specific. There are instructions for almost any problem that might arise in the construction of the garment. Read the whole sheet, both sides, before starting to do anything. *Follow the instructions.* This means you must do everything you are told to do, *in the order given.* Don't do some part of the job you think looks simple first; take the whole job *step-by-step,* just as outlined.

Take your time. Don't allow yourself to be rushed. If you can't finish a particular part of the job in the time allotted, put the garment away until you have time. Rushing is sure to get you into trouble.

Try to have a large box, such as a dress or suit box, to keep the garment in while you are working on it. After cutting out the garment, refold the pattern and keep it in the box. Keep the large scraps, the seam-binding, the zipper, and whatever else you need to complete the garment, all in the box. At the end of each day, fold the garment and keep it in the box. When you have finished all but the hem, the garment can be put on a hanger.

If you are making a dress with a skirt cut on the *bias,* hang all the sections of the skirt from a hanger for two or three days before sewing the skirt seams. Pin them together at the waistline and place over a wire hanger—you may have to pin them to keep them from falling off. This will give the fabric a chance to *stretch* and will make the side seams less likely to pull out later.

Work with a good light. Sewing is like reading; you will eventually get a headache if you strain your eyes for a long time. Be able to see what you are doing.

If convenient, tack up the instruction sheet above the work table. In any case, keep it beside you all the time. Keep a wastebasket handy and throw scraps and trimmings directly into it. Cleaning up later will be easier. Don't wear a good wool dress while sewing because lint and threads will accumulate on it. It goes without saying (but I'll say it anyway) that the work table and your hands should always be clean.

Putting It Together

Not every garment is put together the same way. Step-by-step instructions here would not necessarily match the instructions for your particular garment. Only tips for doing various parts of the construction will be included here, because everything else is subject to the needs of the pattern you are using.

Since you made very clear and abundant marks when you cut out your garment, construction will be easy for you. The whole trick of sewing two shaped pieces of fabric together lies in matching notches and dots. If you have marked every notch, every dot, and every symbol, you will find your way along without bewilderment. You will not realize how important these marks are until you try to adjust a cut edge to another cut edge and come out even. If for some reason, you can't find a mark or failed to make it, place the pattern piece over this particular section and make a new mark.

Darts are marked on the pattern in two ways. One way has a line to stitch on, the other has five or seven dots to be matched. If you have dots, push a pin through one side and bring it out through the dot on the other side. Pin with another pin, at right angles to the line you will stitch. After pinning all the dots, baste through them and remove the pins. If you can't crease the folded edge readily, press it lightly before machine-stitching the dart. Remove the basting threads and press the dart flat in the direction indicated on the instruction sheet.

Figure 6. Basting Stitches

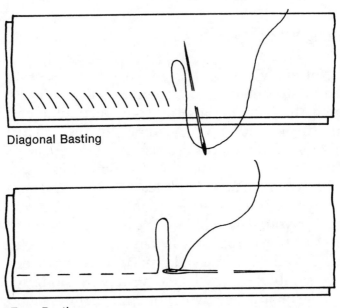

Diagonal Basting

Even Basting

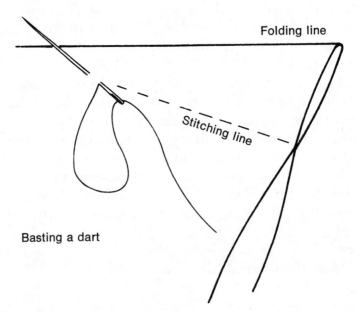

Folding line

Stitching line

Basting a dart

If the dart is marked with lines, fold the material in the center between the two lines and pin in several places along the lines, making sure the pins are on the line on both sides. Baste and stitch.

One thing to look out for in basting darts is the edge of the goods, which would be the underarm seam on a front dart or the neckline in a dart at the back of the bodice. Keep the folded dart even so that the stitching line is continuous right through the finished dart. Keeping the fabric even is the main reason for basting, to keep the fold from shifting while it is being stitched.

You will find from experience that darts are important to the shape of the garment. Those which fit your figure best are the ones which taper to nothing at the highest point of the bust. Because of the great variety of styles, darts vary almost as much as any other part of the garment, so you have to approach darts with a trial-and-error system. By basting and trying on, you can tell if the dart is correct for your figure.

Unless directed otherwise, press every seam as soon as it is stitched. Hand-sewed seams, such as hems, do not necessarily require pressing.

Line up the front and back *shoulder seams* carefully, making sure both ends match; pin and baste. When you have had enough experience to stitch accurately, you will be able to stitch this seam after pinning, without basting.

Sew the *side seams* of a one-piece dress together from the bottom up. Baste this seam to make sure you come out even on top. Keep the stitching straight, because a wobbly seam will not press flat. Side seams on slacks are sewed from bottom up, too. Again, *keep the stitching straight*. Then press.

Sew *skirt seams* together (after putting in the zipper) from the bottom up. Many patterns are marked with the *direction* to stitch indicated on the stitching line; *follow the arrows*.

Don't correct a crooked seam by stitching a straight one over it or next to it; *rip it out*. Two stitchings, even if both of them are straight, will never press flat.

It is time to have a fitting after you have stitched the shoulder and side seams. If you have to make changes, now is the time. Pin up the hem temporarily, because it is impossible to see how the garment will look with an uneven, too-long hemline.

If at this time you decide to take in or let out the side seams, *don't* forget to adjust the sleeve seam or the armhole facing.

If an interfacing is required, for example in the neckline facing, baste the interfacing to the facing and finish the outside edge before sewing the two facings into the neckline. *Always* press zigzag finishes before the final stitching because the zigzag may imprint itself on the right side of the garment if the facing and the right side of the garment are pressed as one.

Baste the facing (and interfacing) to the neckline evenly and use a fairly small stitch when machine-stitching. Accuracy is important here, to insure a symmetrical neckline. Stretch the fabric a *very little* bit when stitching necklines to prevent gathers.

Trim off some of the seam-allowance, leaving about a one-quarter inch margin, and clip the whole neckline on this margin at about one-inch intervals, taking care not to clip the stitching.

Pressing and Over-Stitching

Press. Pressing is so important, in striving for professional results, that it's impossible to stress it too much. Press every seam after stitching. If the steam iron doesn't give satisfactory results, on heavy material, for example, use a clean damp cloth directly on the seam, with a dry cloth on top. Naturally, you must be careful not to press in wrinkles.

When the facing has been stitched, trimmed, and clipped, it is turned inside the garment. Press it carefully all around the opening, carefully maintaining the symmetry of the neckline or armhole. Basting would be recommended if it were not for the fact that the thread can imprint on the finished garment; test your fabric.

Figure 7. Putting in a Facing

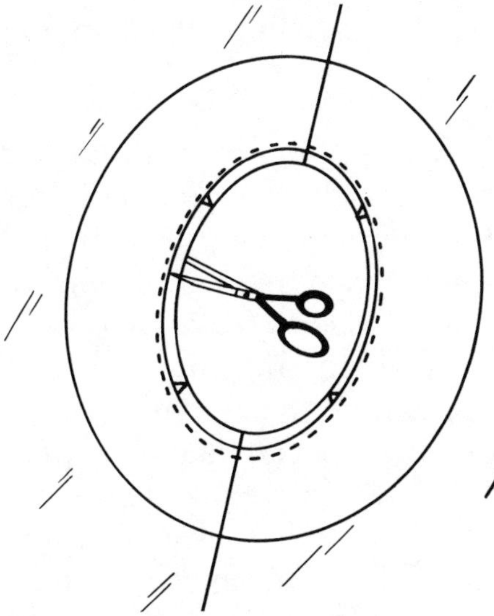

Stitch right sides together and clip    Turn and top-stitch on the right side to prevent rolling.

You can run a line of hand or machine stitching around the inside of neckline and armhole facings, to prevent the facing from showing. Stitch through the facing, the seam-allowance of the facing (and interfacing if any) and the seam-allowance of the neckline. Do this carefully, avoiding stretching the opening out of shape. This is done *after* trimming and clipping. You can also over-stitch directly on the face of the garment, about one-eighth inch from the edge. This visible over-stitching usually looks best if two rows are made, about one-quarter inch apart, with a fairly long stitch.

Sewing in Zippers

If the garment you are making requires a *zipper* or slide-fastener, either in the center front or center back, it is usually easier to sew the fastener in before putting front and back together. The work can be laid out flat on the table while sewing, and pressing is easier too. Zippers in underarm seams can't be done this way, of course.

First make sure you buy the right *size* and *kind* of zipper for your dress. There are zippers which do not separate at the top, for underarm seams; naturally such zippers won't work for skirts and necklines. Always read the instructions on the package. Not only will the instruction help in selection but they also give the simplest method for sewing in the zipper.

Invisible zippers require a special machine part that is not included with the accessories of the sewing machine. Buy a set of the parts the first time you buy an invisible zipper and keep them in the sewing box. Sewing in invisible zippers is different from sewing in regular zippers. You may have to practice once or twice to make sure the two sides of the garment *line up perfectly* at the end of the zipper, after it has been stitched in. Since there is no basting or pressing before the actual installation, the invisible zippers are easy to use once you get the knack. They are good on medium-weight fabrics and on fairly heavyweight fabrics, but very thin goods will not support them. Indeed, very thin material is not suitable for any zipper; use very small *snap fasteners*. If it is possible to put in a fine zipper, sew it in *by hand*.

To insert a regular zipper, baste the seam with the longest stitch on the machine. Finish both edges with zigzag or hand overcasting and press the edges first, then press the seam open lightly. Leave *no less* than five-eighths inch seam-allowance.

If for some reason you do not have adequate seam-allowance or the material ravels a lot or is lightweight, sew two strips of seam binding to the edges of the seam-allowance before sewing in the zipper. Press the tape before pressing open the seam.

You will note that when the zipper is closed, there is about three-quarters of an inch of tape above the slide. You can trim some of this off or turn it back, inside the seam. Usually, the top of the seam is finished off with one hook-and-eye to keep this small gap closed.

Zippers are often sewed in by hand in very expensive tailored garments. This is especially good for underarm zippers, since this is often a curved seam where it is hard to get the zipper to lie perfectly flat while stitching. Baste the seam together as usual, and press lightly. Finish the cut edges as usual. Lay the zipper in place, face down on the wrong side, and baste close to the edge of the tape. Turn the garment right-side-out and stitch about one-quarter inch from the center of the basted seam. Take small stitches, stitching in one place about every three or four stitches, to make sure the sewing is secure. After removing the

Figure 8. Inserting a Zipper

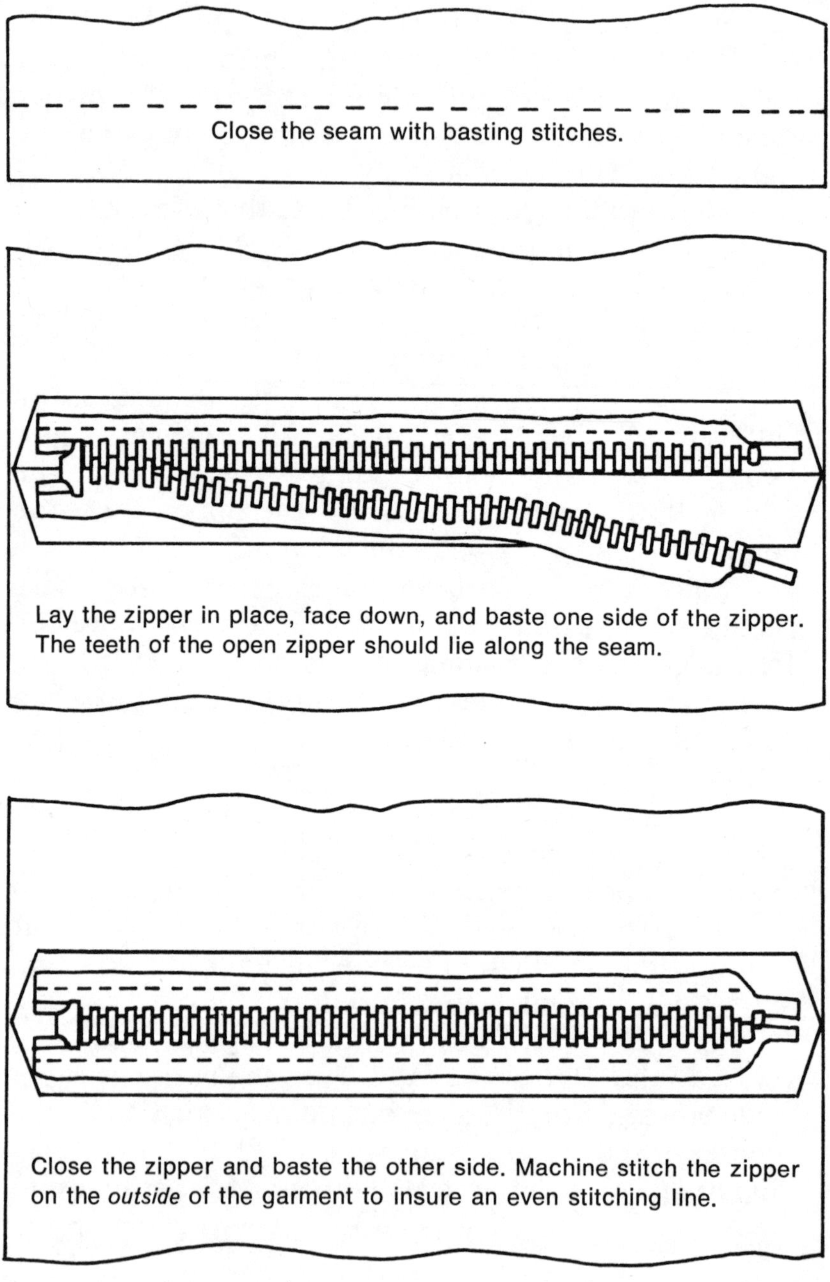

Close the seam with basting stitches.

Lay the zipper in place, face down, and baste one side of the zipper. The teeth of the open zipper should lie along the seam.

Close the zipper and baste the other side. Machine stitch the zipper on the *outside* of the garment to insure an even stitching line.

basting, stitch the edge of the tape on the inside, taking up the seam-allowance so you don't sew through to the face of the dress. This will give you *two lines* of stitching, but only one visible on the outside.

When machine-stitching the zipper, use the *zipper-foot* or the *cording-foot* in place of the regular presser-foot. These gadgets make it possible to sew the correct distance from the zipper teeth which are too thick for the regular foot to pass over. Avoid stitching too close to the teeth. The finished seam will not look good if the stitching is too close, and you may have to detour when you get to the top and have to stitch past the slide. Baste the loose ends of the zipper tape together just above the slide before stitching to help keep them in place and the stitching lines parallel.

9

Stitches, Hems, and Finishes

Overstitching has been used to finish the hem of Tony's shirt. The shirt is a red, purple, and blue print.

9

Stitches, Hems, and Finishes

The instruction book with your sewing machine will show which switch or attachment to use to make *zigzag* stitching. You will discover many uses for this professional-looking finish.

For a neat appearance and to avoid raveling, zigzag all cut edges. You can do this immediately after cutting out the garment or wait until you have sewed the seams. If you do it first, *don't* zigzag the *hem*, the *armholes*, or the *top* of the *sleeve*.

Hand Overcasting, although it takes longer, can be done in place of zigzag if your machine does not make this stitch.

Pinking is not a stitch, but it is done with a special scissors. It makes a neat inside appearance and reduces raveling.

Hemmed Seams are made by turning under about one-eighth inch or less of the seam-allowance and stitching this edge closely. This is not recommended for fabrics thin enough to see through.

French Seams are for very thin material like chiffon, voile, sheers, and others transparent fabrics. The fabric is pinned and basted together as usual, except that *wrong sides* are placed together. Instead of the usual *five-eighths inch* seam-allowance, this seam has *three-eighths inch* margin. You will have to measure from the cut edge occasionally as you baste to keep the seam-allowance uniform. Use a slightly larger stitch for this seam than you would use normally for chiffon, to avoid puckering. Trim the seam, after light pressing, to one-eighth inch. Turn the seam inside out and baste flat, leaving one-quarter inch seam-allowance.

This kind of seam is good for underarm seams, skirt seams, and sleeve seams but not for sewing sleeves into armholes. Sewing the skirt to the waist of a dress made from chiffon or other sheer fabric will not require a special seam if a belt or sash is to be worn. If there is no belt, this seam and the armhole have to have *Bound Seams*.

Bound Seams are started like the usual seam; pin, baste, and stitch, leaving five-eighths inch seam allowance. Make a second stitching close to the first, in the seam allowance. Trim off the seam-allowance close to the second stitching. (This can be zigzagged for a waistline seam.) Cut bias strips of the same material, *one inch wide.* Measure the seam to be bound; if it's an armhole, join the strip to make a continuous band; for a waistband, allow enough at the ends to turn under. Fold the strip lengthwise and baste it to the seam to be bound. Allow one-quarter inch of material on each side of the basting. Stitch it and trim off the raw edge close to the stitching. Turn the folded edge over the seam-allowance. Hand-stitch the folded edge to the other side of the seam-allowance, using a blind stitch. This binding should entirely cover the seam and the seam-allowance. Because the bias strip will stretch a little as you turn it over the seam-allowance, one-quarter inch of fabric will be adequate if you have trimmed the seam-allowance closely.

Before tackling this job, which must be done with precision, it is a good idea to practice on a couple of scraps, to determine the right thread weight, the right stitch length, and the exact width of the bias strip to make the smallest binding possible.

Kinds of Stitches

Stay-Stitching prevents stretching of certain parts of the garment during the sewing process. Stay-stitch as soon as possible after cutting out the garment, before you start to handle the separate pieces much. If the fabric is thin, pin a sheet of tissue paper over the section of the garment requiring stay-stitching and stitch through the paper. Pin all around the edges and in several places in the center to hold the piece as firmly as possible while you are handling it.

Each layer of fabric is stitched separately, of course. Sew next to the stitching line, *in the seam-allowance,* using a medium-length stitch. Avoid stretching the material while working. If the pattern calls for seam-binding or straight tape reinforcing for the stay-stitching, baste it on before machine-stitching.

Shirring can be done three ways; by hand, with the attachment which comes with the sewing machine, and by pulling up or gathering straight stitching.

Hand Shirring is generally used only for short sections of a sleeve, for example, before basting into the armhole, or for baby clothes, lingerie, or any garment where the emphasis is on handwork. Tiny, even, and straight stitches are used, and very fine thread because this is usually a delicate fabric. Otherwise, on the sleeve or where the hand shirring is a part of the construction, this stitching is ripped out after the machine stitching secures it in place.

The shirring attachment on the sewing machine is used where a *miniature pleat* effect is wanted, rather than regular shirring or gathering. Ruffles, which are hemmed top and bottom before shirring, are easily gathered with the attachment. The size of the pleat is adjustable and the spacing is determined by the length of the machine stitch. A certain amount of arithmetic is required to establish the length of the finished section of shirring; absolute accuracy is not guaranteed, so you have to experiment if you have to fit the shirred piece to another piece of the garment. For this reason, it is easier to gather the top of a full skirt with straight stitching.

For a short section of shirring, the bottom of a full sleeve to be finished with a cuff, for example, first complete the binding of the placket. Trim off the ravelings and zigzag the raw edge of the bottom; press the placket, the underarm seam and the zigzag. Adjust the machine tension so the top (needle) thread lies loosely on top of the fabric. (See the instruction manual with the machine.) Use the longest stitch.

Starting next to the placket binding, on the right side of the material, place a row of stitching parallel to the raw edge, about three-quarters of an inch from the edge. Sew a second row about one-quarter of an inch up from the first. Leave three or four inches of thread on both sides of both rows.

Working first from one end and then from the other, pull the top threads, both rows at once, gathering up the fabric as you pull. *Take care* not to break the thread. When the sleeve has been gathered until it is the right size to fit the cuff, stick pins into the two ends of the shirring and wrap the threads around them to secure the threads. Adjust the gathers so that they are even all around. When the shirring fits perfectly, pin and baste the sleeve to the cuff, right sides together. Remove the pins which secured the shirring threads and pull the top threads to the inside (wrong side) of the sleeve.

After machine-stitching the cuff to the sleeve, trim off the zigzagged edge. The second row of shirring stitches will show on the right side after the cuff is turned and finished. Or the shirring stitches can be ripped out if you prefer.

For long sections of shirring, such as on the waistline of a skirt, the procedure is similar but there are a few other things to do to make it easy.

Finish the placket opening as directed on the pattern (sew in the zipper, if any), trim and zigzag the raw edge, and press everything. Mark the notches at *Center Front, Center Back* and each underarm seam with contrasting thread. Tie the thread securely so it won't come out as you work. Make the two rows of stitching as directed above.

Start to shirr the skirt from both ends of the stitching, and from the other three points marked with thread. Pick up the top thread at these points by inserting the blunt end of a needle under a stitch and gently lifting it, pulling carefully until you can get a grip on the thread with the fingers. Shirr from these points as well as from the two ends until the waistband size has been reached. After you have secured all the top threads with pins, the gathers can be pushed back and forth until they are even all the way around.

When the correct size is reached, the top threads are cut and pulled through to the inside and tied. The shirring is then adjusted to cover the loss of these single stitches.

This takes some care, to prevent breaking the thread. Be gentle. Use a little heavier thread than the one used for sewing the rest of the garment. If the thread breaks, rip it out, press the fabric, and start over. *Don't ever try to patch up shirring,* even on shorter sections. Shirring must be done with one thread or gaps appear where they aren't wanted.

From this point on, the skirt is handled much like the sleeve. Pin and baste the shirring to the bodice or waistband, trim off the zigzag (if it is not too stiff, leave it inside the waistband or around the waist if the bodice is zigzagged separately), and machine-stitch. Again, the second row of shirring stitching can show or be removed.

Skirts can be shirred with three or more rows of stitching, too. This gives a flat effect and works well if a belt is to be worn at the waistline.

Easing refers to the process of sewing two edges of fabric together without gathering when one edge is longer than the other. The longer edge is bias or off the straight grain of the fabric, so the easing is accomplished by pushing the fabric together on the diagonal grain of the weave. A line of basting is run on the stitching line of the longer edge and the thread is pulled up gently until the longer edge has been compressed to the length of the shorter one. This is not difficult and requires only that the wrinkles and puckers which form be flattened out. It is advisable to baste the two edges together at this point, and then machine-stitch. Steaming the longer edge will help to shrink out the wrinkles, especially in woolen fabrics.

The opposite of easing is *stretching.* This is done

Figure 9. Stitches and Finishes

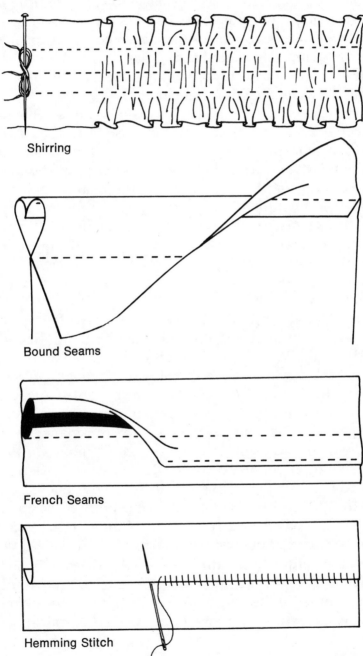

Shirring

Bound Seams

French Seams

Hemming Stitch

while machine stitching. One layer of material must be stretched slightly as the two layers are being joined. The layer to be stretched is usually a short section of a longer seam and should be marked clearly with tailor's tacks to avoid continuing the stretching beyond the exact location indicated.

Basting is temporary sewing, usually done by hand with a needle and thread. Its purpose is to hold two parts of a garment together until they can be sewed permanently. Basting can also be done with the machine, using the longest stitch or the chain-stitch attachment, but this kind of basting is useful to the beginning seamstress only on long straight stretches. Setting a sleeve into the armhole, for example, must be done *by hand*, after pinning; the curve of the top of the sleeve must be *eased* into place with some care to eliminate wrinkles.

Neck and armhole facings, collars, cuffs, pockets, and trimmings should be basted by hand. Spend time basting to save time ripping.

Fit the basting stitch to the situation; on curves, use small stitches close together; on straight stretches, use longer ones. Basting with thread the same color as the garment has one advantage—if by chance you don't get all the bastings out, they won't show. On the other hand, if you use a contrasting color, the basting thread is easier to see to remove. Take your choice.

Always rip out machine basting before the final pressing, because two rows of machine stitching can never be pressed open satisfactorily.

Grain refers to the direction of the threads in the weave—crosswise or lengthwise. Grain is important for a number of reasons, the most important one being that most textiles hang well only with the grain running up and down, or *lengthwise*. Patterns are marked with arrows on every piece: *Straight of Goods* or *Place on Fold*. The *fold* is the lengthwise fold of the fabric; *straight of goods* is straight with the lengthwise grain.

If for some reason it is desirable to make a garment *crosswise* of the grain, be consistent and don't combine both directions unless you have determined that the "hang" of the garment will not be adversely affected. Knits are susceptible to different degrees of stretch in crosswise and lengthwise directions. The difference in the final appearance of the garment is great.

Until you are familiar with the various properties of fabrics, follow the arrows. If there is no stripe to guide you when laying out the pattern, measure from the selvage to both ends of the arrows, to make sure they are all parallel. The importance of keeping to the *straight of the goods* cannot be overemphasized.

Bias refers to a line *diagonal* to the grain of the weave. Most fabrics other than knits do not stretch much in either direction but all will stretch on the bias. (Except non-woven materials like felt and Pellon; since these have no grain at all, they have no bias.) *Never* disregard instructions to cut a particular part of a garment *on the bias*—always follow directions referring to the grain of material.

Never attempt to *bind* anything with strips of fabric *not* cut on a true bias. You will be wasting your time. The exception to this would be an absolutely straight edge, which could be bound with absolutely straight strips. Bias strips would be easier to handle, however, since they stretch. And of course, they will follow curves where straight strips cannot.

To cut true bias, fold a large square of paper into a

right triangle; place one short side of the triangle
against a selvage or any perfectly straight-with-the-
grain edge; mark the fabric parallel to the long side of
the triangle. Move the triangle along the straight edge
and mark as many lines as you need—don't trust your
eye to follow one line when cutting another line. Press
the fabric before marking it.

Hem Finishes

After the hem of a garment has been marked for
length, turned up and trimmed evenly all around, it
can be finished off in various ways, before blind-stitching the hem by hand.

On thin and medium-weight washable material,
turn back about one-quarter inch of the raw edge of
the hem and machine-stitch close to the folded edge.
Press this stitching and hand hem the garment. This is
good for most washable fabrics, even silk, if the result
is not bulky. Linen and wool are too heavy for this
method.

Seam binding can be bought in colors matching or
harmonizing with most woolens and linens. It is
woven with a straight grain and will not stretch—both
edges are selvage. To apply seam binding, open the
hem out flat and lay the seam binding over the raw
edge, lapping about one-quarter inch, and either
straight machine stitch or zigzag close to the edge of
the binding. Press this edge before refolding the hem,
to avoid imprinting the binding on the face of the garment. Hand hem the garment.

Lace edging, one-half to three-quarters inch wide,
can be used in place of seam binding on delicate fabrics. Any narrow *woven braid* in the right weight can

be used, particularly in a garment lined with a contrasting color, where the braid and the lining are coordinated to give a little zip to the inside.

When making hems in heavy material, especially wool, a strip of interlining is sometimes put inside the hem. This is composed of a three- or four-inch wide bias strip, either laid with one raw edge next to the fold of the hem, inside the fold, or basted flat over the fold and folded as one with the hem. This interlining should be loosely blind-stitched in place at both edges, taking care not to make such deep stitches that they show on the face of the garment.

Use an interlined hem on heavy silks, linen, and wool. Knits should have bias strips of cotton or synthetic, preshrunk of course, but for the others, nonwoven materials like Pellon can also be used. Fabrics from the scrap bag can be used; make sure they are true bias. The strips need not be sewed together, but can be lapped a half-inch wherever needed.

Interlined hems are seldom pressed flat and when the garment is to be dry cleaned, the cleaner should be instructed not to do so.

The Mechanics of Hemming

Skirt Hems. Try on the dress and mark the length. The marking can be done with several devices available in notions departments, or with the help of another person. If you purchase one of the marking devices, make sure it will hem very short skirts as well as longer ones. If you are tall and wear a mini-skirt, the marker will have to reach from the floor up to twenty-nine or more inches.

In any case, you will make a *line* around the lower

edge of the skirt, either with *chalk* or *pins*. Turn this hem up inside and baste lightly near the line of pins. Try the dress on once more to make sure you like the length.

Hems look best between two and three inches wide, but if you think you might later want to lengthen this garment, you could make the hem wider. Make a strip of cardboard the width you want for the hem and mark the fold all around, using this gauge to keep it even. Trim off the excess material.

You will notice that the lower edge of the dress is slightly larger than the place where you are going to stitch the hem. Take up this slight excess when sewing on the seam binding. The best way to do this is to baste before stitching. Use a zigzag or straight stitch, fairly long. Press the seam binding after stitching and baste the hem.

Try the dress on for a final look, to determine if the hem is exactly straight. If you think you want the hem a little flatter, press very lightly near the edge, but don't press over the seam binding. Hand-hem the edge and remove the basting.

The usual stitch for a hem is a simple running *blind stitch*. The main thing is that this hem should show as little as possible on the right side of the goods. Use a short hem needle and a single thread to match the fabric. If the material is a print, use a color like the most prominent color of the print.

Start at the seam-allowance. Take a few stitches close together, taking in both the seam binding and the dress goods, then take a stitch in the dress itself, picking up two or three of the threads of the fabric. Push the point of the needle under the free edge of the seam binding and out through the face, catching in about one-eighth of an inch of the seam binding.

Pull the thread through loosely and take the next stitch in the dress, still catching two or three strands of the dress, about one-half inch from the first stitch. Make all the stitches in the dress the same size, that is, taking up the same number of strands of the goods and spaced the same distance apart. Keep them in a straight line, just under the edge of the seam binding.

As you work, you will hold the garment in front of you with the folded edge of the hem to your left. You may then take your stitches towards yourself, down, or away from yourself, up. Try both directions and see which is easier for you. Or you can lay the work crosswise in front of you and work towards either your left or right, whichever is easier.

The other way to make this hem stitch, not quite so "blind" but equally effective, is to take the first part of the stitch in the seam-binding, pushing the needle through from the back, then pulling up the thread and taking the stitch in the fabric, again picking up only two or three strands of yarn. If you use this method, you will be picking up threads from the dress goods which run up-and-down, whereas, in the first method, you tend to pick up crosswise threads. If you experiment with your fabric, you will see which is easier and which makes the best-looking stitch on the right side.

A hem in the bottom of slacks is made this way, unless the slacks are lined. The bottom of a blouse can be done this way if the material is fairly heavy; if the material is light, no seam binding is used. The bottom edge of the blouse is turned back about one-quarter inch and stitched close to the edge; this is then turned to the required length and hemmed.

There are a few things which can help to prolong the good appearance of hems; do not press them hard at any time, either when pressing or ironing. Always repair a hem at once when it begins to rip. If the edge shows wear, let out the whole hem and turn it up about half an inch; this slightly shorter length will not be noticed and it will improve the look of the whole dress. This should be done with sleeves, if they show wear, too, although it is usually not possible with slacks.

Hems in *children's clothes* present a special problem. To prolong the life of the garment it is desirable to let down hems as the child grows. Most washable fabrics fade a little, both from repeated laundering and from exposure to light; the turned-under part of the hem fades less than the rest of the garment. Furthermore, the edge of the hem wears more than the rest of the garment and a worn line appears when the hem is let out.

One possibility for correcting this problem is to make the dress or slacks, at least for girls' slacks, with some sort of trim, like rickrack. Naturally, some braid is also used elsewhere on the dress: around the neck, on the sleeves, or on the collar, for example.

Determine the length of the garment and mark a line where the hem will be folded. If the dress has a two-inch hem, it can be let down once to increase the length two inches; this is about right for school-age children, who grow at a slower rate than toddlers. This method is not suitable if the hem has to be wider than three inches.

Mark lines two inches above and below the *foldline* of the hem. There should be another two inches of fabric below this bottom line. Stitch the rickrack on these three lines. Fold under the two inches of fabric below the bottom row and fold the hem on the middle row, letting the braid show outside. Hem the dress under the top row of rickrack, and when it is necessary to let down the hem, open up the turned-under fabric, and hem again behind the middle row of rickrack.

This method, while it does not eliminate sun fading, will eliminate the worn line, which will be behind the rickrack, and will allow up to three inches increase in the dress length.

For material that will not fade, two or three rows of tucks in the skirt above the hem make possible another method of lengthening. One or two tucks can be let down as the child grows. Machine stitching leaves a line but when the tuck is let out, a row of lace, rickrack, or other trim can be sewed on or a line of machine embroidery can be made to cover the marks. This is very attractive on young children's clothes and makes it possible to use "good" dresses for a longer time, and for more than one little girl.

The best way to get around the unsightly line from let-out tucks is to sew the tucks in by hand, since hand stitching leaves less conspicuous marks than machine stitching. Three rows of one-inch tucks may look better than one three-inch tuck; they can be let out one at a time as the need arises. However, one hand-sewed three-inch tuck can be ripped out, washed, pressed, and replaced by a two-inch tuck. The second method eliminates stitching marks a little better than the three-tuck method.

In either case, press tucks as little as possible to prevent "setting" the folded edge. Let the garment out promptly as the child grows. It is better to lengthen a dress twice than to let out a wide hem all at once, especially if it is sun faded.

10

Lining the Garment

A dress and jacket such as Vina's should be lined for shape and comfort. The outfit is made of brown linen, with a white yoke on the dress.

10

Lining the Garment

There are two basic types of *lining*. One is made entirely separate from the garment it lines and is sewed in after both have been constructed. This kind of lining is found in coats and suit jackets and is the product of that complicated process known as "tailoring," which is not what this book is all about.

Nevertheless, there are times when a lining is wanted in a garment not exactly "tailored" in the strictest sense. For a beginner to handle this problem, to even consider it, certain ground rules have to be followed.

First, it must be a *very simple* pattern. No collar, no complex shaping, no two-piece sleeve, no funny business. The jacket fabric must be medium weight; the lining fabric must be easy to handle, keep its shape, and be lighter than the jacket. Really heavy materials make lumpy garments unless they are properly tailored.

Since the pattern is simple, both the jacket and the lining will be easy to put together; the problem comes when they are joined. The jacket, complete with its front and neck facings, is pressed carefully. The hem has been basted in. The sleeves have been sewed in and the hems turned up to the correct length and basted.

The lining back and the two parts of the front are sewed together and the seams pressed. The sleeves are sewed in but not pressed. The seam-allowance need not be trimmed but curves should be clipped. The pleat in the center back of the lining is basted in place but not pressed down.

There is no neck or front facing to the lining. Turn under the seam-allowance on both the front and the neckline and baste close to the fold. Clip carefully at the curves of the neckline but not deep enough to reach the fold. Do not press this edge.

Turn the jacket inside out without turning the sleeves inside out and lay the lining, right side up, on to the jacket, matching the shoulder seams of the lining to the shoulder seams of the jacket neck and front facings. Pin the lining to the facing, lapping the facing just the width of the seam-allowance, i.e., five-eighths of an inch, from each shoulder seam across the back of the neck. Pin close together, with the pins at right angles to the edge of the lining. Then pin down the two fronts, matching the notches of the lining with notches in the facing. Do not stretch either the lining or the jacket facing.

Baste the lining to the facings, keeping the facing free from the jacket front so that you do not baste through to the outside of the jacket. Put your hand under the lining and hold the facing up while basting.

Turn the jacket right-side-out again and stuff the sleeve lining into the jacket sleeves. Turn up the lining, making it about one-half inch shorter than the jacket. You may have to trim the lining, for you should have no more than a one-inch hem in the bottom or the sleeve. The sleeve lining, however, should be long enough to have about one-half inch excess length to prevent it from binding, even though it will be sewed to the inside of the jacket sleeve about one inch up from the hem.

Try on the jacket to see if the lining shows below the jacket and if the sleeve lining is too tight.

Hand-stitch the Lining

You can go either of two ways from here. You can blind-stitch the lining by hand on both front facings and around the neck. You can blind-stitch the sleeve lining to the turned-under sleeve hem, and hand-hem the lining, which hangs loose from the jacket. This is the customary procedure and by far the easiest way to finish the lining.

However, there is another way and you might prefer it. Turn the lining inside out, without turning the sleeves, and baste all around the jacket front and neck facing, basting together the lining seam-allowance and the facing seam-allowance. After this basting is finished, the first basting, the one which placed the lining on the facing, is removed and the two edges are machine-stitched together, taking up the full five-eighths inch seam-allowance.

Basting this is not easy. It is possible that you may have to make a third basting, after removing the first one, to make sure you can take up the full seam-allowance when you machine-stitch, without shifting the lining. Use a long stitch on the machine and do not remove basting until you are satisfied with the results of the final stitching.

Either way, of course, you will *hand-hem* both the

3

bottom of the jacket and the bottom of the lining. The sleeve lining will be *blind-stitched* by hand to the turned-up hem of the jacket sleeve. This sleeve hem need not be sewed before the lining is sewed in. The jacket hem can have a seam-binding finish if you wish, or it can be zigzagged; the lining hem should not be seam-bound but it can be zigzagged. This is a good place to use a strip of bias interfacing laid inside the jacket hem and the hem on the sleeve, before sewing in the lining.

Lining Sewed as One

The other kind of lining is sewed as one with the fabric of the garment. It is used to add body to limp material, to help prevent stretching and sagging, and sometimes to back up transparent or open-work materials like eyelet or lace. *Si Bonne*, a synthetic-fiber lining in two or three different weights, is used with silk, other synthetics, and sometimes with linen. Cotton in thin, firm weaves is usually used with linen and other cottons. There are other synthetics such as Celanese and rayon, which are sometimes used, as well as a nonwoven interlining called *Pellon*, which is used to line skirts where a stiff effect is desired.

Linings sewed as one with the garment are not very hard to handle, if the right fabric is used for the lining. The lining fabric should complement the weight or "hand" of the face fabric. A garment which is going to be laundered should be preshrunk, both fabric and lining, because few sets of lining and face fabric can be expected to shrink exactly the same amount.

Select the lining when you buy the face fabric and

buy the most economical material that will do the job. On the other hand, don't sacrifice the whole garment for a few pennies, because no matter what you pay for fabrics, the work is still the same. Choose close-grained fabric for lining, without texture or woven design. Since the whole idea of lining is to add body, make sure the lining fabric is firm. Avoid cloth that looks like it might pull apart or be difficult to handle; clinging fabric, on the other hand, can be good if it doesn't stretch.

For transparent face fabrics, you might want to add a dimension by using a lining in a different color, to give a "changeable" effect. Under lace or eyelet, use a good quality material because it is partly face fabric too. With wool, the color is generally not important, since it will not show through the face fabric, but it's fun to use a bright color for lining to give a little excitement to a plain skirt—say bright red under navy, for instance.

The good-quality synthetic knits require no lining. Linen doesn't need it either, but many people like the added body and stiffness. Wool knits can use lining to help prevent sagging, but care must be taken that the seams do not appear rigid, since knits are expected to stretch. The usual solution for this is to line the skirt only.

The best way to do this is to make the lining entirely independently of the skirt, *slightly smaller* through the hips than the face fabric and slightly shorter. Then the lining and the face fabric are sewed together along the stitching line at the waistline and enclosed in a single waistband of the face fabric.

The lining fabric is left open along the opening for

the zipper, which is sewed into the face fabric. The lining material is then turned back and blind-stitched by hand to the inside of the face fabric or the zipper tape.

Cutting and Sewing

Cut out lining the same way you cut face fabric. Mark *darts* and other construction guides exactly the same way. Lay each piece of the lining on the *wrong* side of the corresponding piece of the face fabric and baste accurately along the stitching lines. *Slash* the lining material down the *center line* of darts and baste all darts carefully along the stitching lines before folding the dart and basting in place.

You can zigzag the lining and face fabric together before putting the garment together or wait until the principal seams are stitched. Press the zigzag flat before pressing the seam open to eliminate imprinting. You may want to trim away the lining around darts before pressing them flat, especially if the face fabric is rather heavy.

It is usually not necessary to line *facings* for necklines or armholes, unless the face fabric is very thin or hard to handle. When tacking down facings and blind-stitching the hem, take the hand-stitch through *both layers of material* to prevent stretching the lining away from the face fabric.

Interlining

If the pattern you are using calls for interlining and you don't want extra stiffness in the areas to be interlined, use the lining fabric to interline these

Figure 10. Lining a Skirt

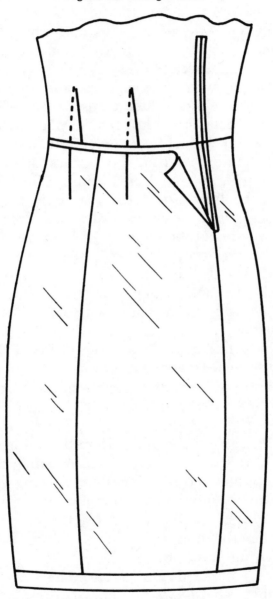

With wrong sides together, put the skirt lining in the dress, attaching the lining to the skirt at the zipper and at the waistline.

places. Some garments really need the stiffness, however, so use your judgment.

There is another way of using lining which is a
combination of these two methods. You can use this
method for a sleeveless dress or blouse made from a
thin nylon jersey or other very thin and clinging fabric
to give it body and reduce transparency. The lining
should be the same kind of fabric; plain nylon tricot
to line printed nylon, for example. Both lining and face
fabric are cut out as usual, both marked as usual. *No*
neck facing is cut from dress or lining fabric.

Make the dress as usual, *omitting* the neck facing.
If a zipper is used, sew it in. Make the lining, which is
another version of the same dress, but take up a *wider
seam-allowance* on the two side seams, reducing the
lining size about three-quarters of an inch. When sewing in the armhole facing for the lining, take up a
larger seam-allowance here too, to make a slightly
larger armhole.

Turn the lining inside out and fit it over the dress,
so that the *right sides* are together.

Pin and baste the two garments together around
the neckline. Stitch, trim and clip this seam and turn
the dress right-side-out. You now have two finished
dresses, one inside the other. Hem the lining one inch
shorter than the outside dress. Blind-stitch the opening in the lining to the zipper tape, using very long
stitches and keeping the stitching loose.

This type of lining is very attractive used with soft
prints when the lining is one of the colors in the print,
or in two different colors when the top material is
transparent or semi-transparent. The dress pattern
should always be *simple.* The outside dress could have

a sleeve, but the lining should still have a faced armhole.

    Now, you have read all about making garments for
yourself and for others in your family. I hope that you
will have as much pleasure sewing as my family has
had through the years. Then, you can make an African
border print (in red, purple, and black) just as Lisi
did and have fun posing in it.